Collector's Encyclopedia of
NIPPON
PORCELAIN

Identification & Values

Fifth Series

Joan F. Van Patten

COLLECTOR BOOKS
A Division of Schroeder Publishing Co., Inc.

The current values of this book should be used only as a guide. They are not intended to set prices, which vary from one section of the country to another. Auction prices as well as dealer prices vary greatly and are affected by condition as well as demand. Neither the Author nor the Publisher assumes responsibility for any losses that might be incurred as a result of consulting this guide.

Searching for a Publisher?

We are always looking for knowledgeable people considered to be experts within their fields. If you feel that there is a real need for a book on your collectible subject and have a large comprehensive collection, contact Collector Books.

On the cover:

Plate 3060: Humidor, white woodland pattern, 6¾" tall, blue mark #47, $825.00 – 925.00
Plate 3015: Urn, gold overlay, 13" tall, blue mark #52, $1,700.00 – 2,000.00
Plate 3049: Vase, 9¾" tall, blue mark #362, $650.00 – 750.00

Cover Design: Terri Stalions
Book Design: Holly C. Long

Additional copies of this book may be ordered from:

Collector Books
P.O. Box 3009
Paducah, Kentucky 42002-3009

@ $24.95. Add $2.00 for postage and handling.

Contents

Dedication

This book is dedicated to all the wonderful Nippon collectors who contributed photographs and information. You made it a reality. My sincere thanks goes to each and every one of you.

About the Author

Joan Van Patten is the author of seven other books published by Collector Books, *The Collector's Encyclopedia of Nippon Porcelain*; *The Collector's Encyclopedia of Nippon Porcelain, Second Series*; *The Collector's Encyclopedia of Nippon Porcelain, Third Series*; *The Collector's Encyclopedia of Nippon Porcelain, Fourth Series*; *Nippon Porcelain Price Guide*, *The Collector's Encyclopedia of Noritake*; and *The Collector's Encyclopedia of Noritake, Second Series*. She has also written numerous trade paper and magazine articles and is a contributor to *Schroeder's Antiques Price Guide*.

She has been on the board of directors of the International Nippon Collectors Club (INCC) since its inception; she served as its first president, and was also the co-founder. She has lectured on the subjects of Nippon and Noritake throughout the United States and Canada. Research, travel, and volunteer work are other major interests of the author.

Acknowledgments

My heartfelt thanks go to Billy Schroeder and the wonderful staff at Collector Books. Billy makes these books a possibility and his company is the most fantastic to work for. I cannot say enough good things about them. Lisa Stroup, my editor and Gina Lage, her assistant, work very hard to make sure these books turn out so well. Thanks to everyone on the staff for their help.

It's been said that "authors are like bees who pillage here and there among the flowers," and I feel a little like one of those bees. I have had the help of so many Nippon collectors. Words alone cannot express my gratitude.

Again, Earl Smith and Mark Griffin have provided wonderful photos, over 150. Their photographer is Clement Photographic Services, Inc. in Ft. Myers, Fla. In my opinion they have the most spectacular Nippon collection known to exist, and I am so happy they were willing to share their beautiful items with other collectors. They also helped with pricing which is a horrendous task. A special thanks goes to these two very special guys.

I used nearly 90 of the beautiful photographs Elwood and Charlene Matlosz sent. Their daughter Michele was their photographer and once again did a super job. The Matlosz family also helped with pricing and I feel they have made a big contribution to this book. Thanks to all three of you.

Bob and Maggie Schoenherr's photos (nearly 70) of their favorite items are a great addition. Many hours were spent preparing for photo taking and writing descriptions and I know collectors will enjoy viewing these photos. Thank you.

Ken Schirm sent batch after batch of items from his collection. I wish I knew where he finds all those eye-popping pieces. He has a great collection and I appreciate all the work he did.

Jess Berry is always there to help — not only with photos but this time with two chapters! A number of his and Gary Graves' items are featured and add immensely to this edition. I know readers are going to be interested in Jess' newest information on dog items and the flying swan pattern. Thank you both.

Judy Boyd also wrote two chapters — one on enameling and the other one dealing with sports portrayed on Nippon wares. This one is really fun reading. She also provided a number of photos. Thanks, Judy, for all your help, but also for being my friend.

Rachel Altounian provided three chapters for readers. She has done a lot of research on Japan and the Morimura family and I am indebted to her once again. Thanks, Rachel, for your help.

Ed and Joan Vanzo provided a very interesting chapter on Nippon designs from the Victorian era to the Art Deco period. They have an awesome collection of condensed milk containers and used them to show readers how the different designs evolved over the years. They also sent photos of some of their favorite pieces which I am pleased to include.

Dennis and Susan Buonafede have managed to amass a breathtaking collection of old Noritake Company salesman pages. When I viewed their Nippon era ones, I was literally brought to tears. They generously consented to have some of them featured in this book. I know readers are going to love seeing the original sketches. This is one of my favorite chapters.

Special thanks go to Osamu (Sam) Tsutsui and the Noritake Company for the remainder of the salesman pages. They gave me copies of nearly 65 from their archives and many of these will be featured in (hopefully) future books. Sam is always so helpful and I really appreciate all he has done.

The Jewel Tea Company information will probably be a surprise to most collectors. I know it was for me. I first made contact with Gwynneth Harrison and she got me in touch with Harriet Kurshadt and Catherine Otto. Gwynn and Catherine related several stories to me and Harriet graciously consented to write the chapter. Thanks go to each of these ladies for their help.

I found myself with a Japanese patent and no way to translate it. Wayne and Mary Myers came to the rescue. It was sent to a friend of theirs in Japan and soon it arrived at my doorstep in English. Thank you both.

Aki Oga from Japan found the patent on Royal Kinjo marked items which we've all wondered about. She translated it and was gracious to share it with readers.

Nat Goldstein purchased a small Nippon-marked cosmetic jar a while back, complete with the original box and instructions. I appreciate the photos he sent on this. Isn't Nippon history fascinating?

Research turned up twenty 1921 patents for Noritake dinnerware. Not knowing the pattern names I consulted the experts, Robert Page, Virginia Piazza, and Peggy Rousch, who identified them from the patent drawings. To date, I have found few Nippon era patents, so these were exciting to locate. Thanks to the experts for their information.

Special gratitude goes to Don and Shirley Bakely who not only sent photos but helped with the pricing for the woodland scene items which is their specialty. The three of us worked diligently on information about these items and perhaps a future book will contain it.

Michael Driban has an extraordinary Nippon collection and sent photos of many pieces. Russ Heckman worked with him on the pricing of these items and thanks goes to both of them for their contribution.

Lee and Donna Call sent many photos and I was

pleased to include over 30 of them in this series. Thanks to both of you for your help.

Lewis and B. J. Longest sent photos of items in their collection and Lewis also took photos for friends. Lewis is a professional photographer and, of course, his photos were impressive. Thanks so much.

Polly Frye, another professional photographer, also sent some exceptional photos of her pieces and she also photographed fellow collectors' items for the book. Thanks, Polly, for your help.

Linda Lau not only sent photos, she also helped with the doll chapter and located two patents for me. We've had a lot of fun trying to figure out the mystery patent, talking about salesman sample pages and the repros. Thanks, Linda.

Thanks go to four fellow Nippon collectors, Reggie Hankin, Ken Harman, Walt Maytan, and Peter Mancanello. They provided some wonderful photos and information, but best of all, they gave their friendship.

Many, many others helped either with photos and/or information and are listed below:

Sam Bourne	Elizabeth Cohee
Chuck Dillon	Becky Federico
Philip Fernkes	Dawn Fischer
Bernadine Knotts	Kenneth Landgraf
Todd and Karen Lawrence	David Lucas
Mike and Rosemary	Scott and Jana Morrison
Mikolajczak	George Murphy
Don Posthumus	Marcia Potts
Jim and Nancy Powers	Paul and Ollys Preo
David Przech	Helen Puckett
David Pullins	Larry Shields
Al Snyder	Alene Svenson
Wendy Van Patten	Duke and Donna Ward
Elmer and Peggy Williams	Marie Young

A generous thank you to each and every person who was part of this project. I couldn't have done it without you! I hope you enjoy the book.

Introduction

"The greatest part of a writer's time is spent in reading in order to write; a man will turn over half a library to make one book." Samuel Johnson

There was no shortcut to my knowledge of Nippon porcelain. When I first began collecting Nippon, there were four small spiral-bound books on the market containing very limited information. Now there are five books in this series showing thousands and thousands of items. And hopefully, they will give readers a jump-start with their education.

Sources of information have been gleaned from many sources. I can remember back to my first book, thinking that it would be the definitive book on the subject. How wrong I was and how much more information we have gained. There is now an International Nippon Collectors Club (INCC) which holds an annual convention and auction as well as publishing six newsletters a year. And today there are thousands of known collectors. What a difference!

Through the use of these five books, readers can be armchair travelers in the wonderful world of Nippon. Hopefully, they will be your passport to knowledge and pleasure.

The first book has photos numbered from 1–366; Second Series has plates 367–1210; the Third Series has plates 1211–2378; and the Fourth Series has plates 2379–2906. All types of new items and decoration are included in the Fifth Series as well as more exciting information and photographs.

When I began collecting in the late '60s, cups and saucers, small candy dishes, and vases were my specialty. I was not aware that there were tapestry items and wedgwood pieces. Blown-out items consisted of the nut dishes. My world was very limited, but with the wares featured in these books and some intense studying (which means reading the text as well as looking at the photos), you can have a first rate collection right away. You won't need to make the mistakes I made. Knowledge is power and collectors now have a wealth of information at their fingertips that collectors just 15 to 20 years ago did not have.

It's been said that the joy of collecting is like a love affair — the headiness of infatuation, the pursuit, and rapture of conquest. Nippon collecting is all this and more; it brings joy, happiness, and excitement to the collector.

Some collections are formed by happenstance, but the true collections have been lovingly gathered over the years. The collecting instinct seems basic to human nature. Some collectors are obsessive, compulsive, and cannot stop. Many are packrats. But I think the "hunt" is almost as desirable to most people as the actual possession of a piece. Nippon collecting is addictive. You have been forewarned. So beware!

The recent years have shown sweeping changes in attitudes towards Nippon. In the '60s and '70s, it was sort of "junk" to many dealers. Now they talk about it in more reverent terms. The quality was always there, the price wasn't. Of course, that is no longer the case.

There are all types of items available for purchase. Some collectors specialize in certain techniques, such as tapestry or moriage, while others may have a large collection of vases and urns or perhaps humidors. Some are eclectic collectors and want a little of everything. No two hand-painted pieces are ever the same. Each is unique. The Japanese factories employed numerous craftsmen to produce these highly decorated pieces.

Edward S. Morse was one of the first foreigners to visit Japan after the country was opened in 1854. In his book *Japan Day By Day*, he tells how he took up the study of Japanese pottery on his second visit in 1882.

He writes that "members of the family are engaged on this work — from the little boy or girl to the old grandfather, whose feeble strength is utilized in some simple process of the work.

"Boys, often ten years old, splashing on the decoration of flowers and butterflies, and the like; motives derived from their mythology, but in sickening profusion so contrary for their own use.

There was the feverish activity of work, with every Tom, Dick and Harry and their children slapping it out by the gross."

I would venture to guess that Mr. Morse did not approve of the western style decoration that we loved both then and now, and I am sure that he could not imagine how in demand it would become.

An assembly line type system was eventually introduced by the Morimuras to keep secret many of the decorating techniques developed at the factory. Previously, workers would be taught by the company masters and often jumped around from factory to factory, taking these skills and secrets with them. In an effort to stop this from happening, it was decided that each worker would only be allowed to do one type of work on the finished product; thus no worker knew it all. Each did a little part of the work and items were passed around to others to do something different. Each worker specialized in his own area of expertise and thus the secrets were kept.

In the late 1890s Rikishi Sato worked for the Morimuras in Nagoya and was considered their outstanding artist. Along with other top artists, the Morimuras were able to turn out high quality work, using many different types of wares and designs.

The Noritake factory was erected on an area of land owned by the very wealthy Noritake family. The Noritakes originally had no dealings with the Morimuras, but the Noritake name was liked so it was placed on their products. This is really not a novel idea, as many local names in Japan have been applied to other products over the years.

Research indicates that glaze effects in use during the early years were:

transparent	transparent shiny
transparent mat	non-transparent mat
non-transparent/opaque	shiny
milky	mat
crystalline	lustre

In an old mid-winter 1916 Larkin catalog, names were ascribed to various patterns advertised for sale. It did not show these patterns, but the names were mountain lake, in the dell, rushing brook, moon reflections, passing clouds, summer evening, moonlight, and golden dawn across the meadow. Can't you just imagine some of these names linked with the designs featured in the Nippon books?

In a December 1908 Butler Bros. catalog, portraits were very popular on china ware. One ad reads "portraits of the empire" and then goes on to list china table plates bearing portraits of Napoleon, Josephine, Marie Louise, Hortense, etc.

Another ad in the same issue was for high grade imported china table plates. This one says that these items have portraits of assorted European beauties and other famous people. On one bowl, Madam LeBrun is featured; another has her daughter's portrait and others have Spanish beauties. Queen Louise was evidently a favorite because she appears often in the ads. Prices ranged anywhere from 35¢ to 95¢ each for these pieces.

A common question heard from novice collectors is, "What shall I collect?" My reply is first, buy what you like and also buy what you can afford. But always remember, one good item is always better than purchasing two or three mediocre pieces. Buy quality wares. Inferior workmanship lessens the value and desirability.

Missing lids, cracks or chips, and extensive gold wear all have a bearing on price, or at least they should. Collectors like to share their knowledge with others, so ask questions of other collectors and dealers. Read the books. Join the INCC and attend its conventions. You will see more pieces of Nippon in one place than you can ever imagine. Familiarize yourself with the reproductions so that you can tell them apart from the genuine wares.

There's a Japanese proverb that says "By searching the old, learn the new." And so it is with our quest for Nippon.

Pricing

Price guides are always controversial and I expect the prices listed in this book to be no exception. Collectors and dealers must realize that these prices are merely a starting point in determining a price and are not intended to set them. They are to be used only as a guide.

You will find estimated retail prices listed. Every piece is considered to be in mint condition, not cracked or chipped, with no extensive gold ware, no repairs, etc. Adjustments in price should always be made when an items is not in pristine condition. Each piece should be judged on its own merit and workmanship.

Collectors should buy what appeals to them regardless of what the collecting trends are at the moment. Fads come and go. What is in favor today may not command as high a price a few years from now. Other items may skyrocket.

Auction fever overcomes many collectors and drives up prices on certain items to all-time highs. This does not mean that this should now be the price for all similar items. Two spirited bidders may have gotten carried away and the high price is the result of the auction and who wanted the item the most or who had the deepest pockets. I've been to many auctions when really good items went far below what I thought they should have. Again, this does not set the price. Buyers for that particular pattern or item may not have been in the audience.

Prices reflect several things — demand, quality of workmanship and artistry, scarcity, the condition of the item, collecting fads, and the desire of the buyer as well as the size of the pocketbook. Prices vary in different localities, regional tastes differ, and the price often is based on the margin of profit the dealer wants. Items may be priced according to what was paid for the piece or a dealer's estimation on what it will bring in a particular market. If a collector wants something badly enough, he will probably be willing to pay more than others.

Collectors should look for quality and buy what they like. Good Nippon is out there; we just need a good dose of patience.

Many people helped with this price guide. I never set prices by myself although I am ultimately responsible for those decisions. The more you shop for Nippon, the more you'll be able to disregard price guides and rely on your own knowledge as to what is the correct price. Five people can give an estimated price for what I may think is a $1,000 item and the five prices will often be all across the board. This does not make any of them wrong; it just proves what an impossible task pricing can be.

Study the books and you'll get an idea of what is more expensive and what are everyday finds. Don't pay a premium price for an ordinary item. But whatever you do, enjoy your collecting. Whoever said that money can't buy happiness doesn't know where to shop for Nippon!

U.S. Exportation of Nippon Porcelain

By Rachel Altounian

The Consul-General's Report

At the Philadelphia Centennial Exposition of 1876, the Japanese had over 17,000 square feet of display space, including porcelains which not only received awards, but were found to be irresistible art objects by Americans. In May of 1877, Tiffany & Co. of New York exhibited "the rarest specimens of Satsuma porcelain... plates with scalloped edges with the Imperial Chrysanthemum... and exquisite bits of enamel on porcelain." A *New York Times* article described it, "The whole side of Fifteenth Street is invaded by the Japs." Americans were fascinated by the artwork of "rediscovered" Japan, and created a demand for Japanese hand-painted porcelain.

Being an astute marketing analyst of his time, Baron Morimura, the largest exporter of Nippon porcelain, saw this demand for Japanese porcelain growing in the U. S. and promptly capitalized on it. Out of eight Japanese import-export businesses that set up shop in the U. S. at that time, only his survived.

Kanagawa, Japan, (later named Yokohama), in 1881, was a spacious and accessible bay city, with a population of 80,000. It was known for good anchorage and most favorable shipping conditions. Under the 1854 Treaty of Kanagawa, diplomatic agents from the United States obtained the rights to dwell in the ports open to commerce and establish consulates. A fixed territorial colony was given to Americans under jurisdiction of its own Consul-General. Americans had freedom of religion there, and enjoyed freedom of trade only with the payment of a fixed tariff of five percent of their value of exported goods. Close to 70 percent of Japan's exports were shipped from Kanagawa, and there were 253 Americans with 27 firms set up for direct trade to San Francisco. By comparison, the treaty-port of Kobe-Osaka had nine American firms and Nagasaki had only three. Kanagawa could be reached from Tokyo by rail in an hour, but Americans needed special permission to travel outside their treaty limits.

Japanese porcelain for export was in its early stages of development. Transportation facilities needed to be improved to transport raw materials to the manufacturers and finished products to the ports. Japan gradually increased and improved upon its porcelain exports by continued development of industrial art and labor productivity. The United States had a significant role in increasing the output and improving the quality of export porcelain, which meant greater profits for the manufacturers.

From 1874 to 1882, the U. S. Consul-General stationed in Kanagawa was Thomas B. Van Buren. A native of Englewood, New Jersey, his duties were to oversee the judicial rights of U. S. citizens living and working in Kanagawa, report the volume of imports from and exports to the U. S., and maintain peaceful and cooperative relations with the Japanese officials. Although his terms in office raised much controversy over supposed "immoral and scandalous practices and cruel sentences" against U. S. Naval officers, he was respected and known to be a great humanitarian in bridging the gap between Americans and the Japanese. This apparently caused much jealousy among his political peers in the U. S., who maliciously slandered his reputation to the press. Nevertheless, Van Buren earned respect from the Japanese.

He was especially concerned with the pottery and porcelain industries, personally touring the porcelain factories, studying their methods and volume of annual production. In November of 1880, he visited the porcelain manufacturers in the village of Seto. Seeing the need for improvements in production, quality, and transportation, he made specific suggestions. They were carried through with great satisfaction and gratitude from the manufacturers. As a result, production expenses were lowered, quality improved, and profits increased. In 1881, Van Buren wrote a detailed report on the pottery and porcelain industries of Japan, which was recognized in the *New York Times*, and could very well have helped open up larger markets.

The Morimura Porcelain Factory

By Rachel Altounian

Finding the following description of the Morimura factory was like discovering a $250 Nippon vase at a garage sale for $20. Surely some of you collectors have experienced that rarity, or maybe something close to it!

In *Japan at First Hand*, a book written by Joseph I. C. Clarke in 1918, the author describes in detail his visit to Japan. His account is well written, and gives a very sensitive and scholarly understanding of Japanese society. Regarding porcelain, he denounces the inferior export wares made by obscure factories. He describes one porcelain factory in Osaka as a small, stodgy factory "turning out their stint of product amid dusty, ill-kempt surroundings...things for the common market done in a common way."

In contrast, he mentions that the Morimura porcelain factory manufactures high quality porcelain, and he is obviously impressed by their production facility:

At Nagoya, I went through the large Morimura porcelain factory, where 2,500 hands are employed, who work from 6 a.m. to 6:30 p.m., with time for meals. Perhaps half are young women. We were shown the entire process from the puddling of the kaolin or porcelain clay through the shaping and wheel-work and the baking, glazing and painting. The shops are large and airy, and there is an American air of briskness not usually visible in the crafts work of Japan.

A large part of their business is of the smaller order of things for the cheaper grades of porcelain. One order amused me, namely, 1,400 cases of cups and saucers for 700 "ten cent stores" in the United States. Each case contains 300. So that these enterprising merchants of Uncle Sam account for 420,000 cups and saucers from Nagoya every year. What a mighty flood of gossip over the ten-cent tea cups this fact pre-figures! They have a large trade with England also in like ware and competed successfully with Germany.

Modern English shaping machinery is used on a great scale. In the painting department I saw one hundred men, youths and girls painting the colors by hand on several pieces of excellent quality. Designs are furnished by special artists. These are outlined on black on paper for them and the patterns are applied over the plaque, plate, cup or vase, wetted and then taken off leaving the design outlined on the object. The color artist then paints on the design in colors, sometimes varying it a little. Some of the plaques were excellent.

We also saw hollow casting in dry plaster moulds. A fluid mixture of kaolin and water is poured into the dry mould, which absorbs the water and attracts the kaolin, which settles in a thin flake on the mould. The water is poured off, and mould and all put in the oven and baked.

There is a large dining hall for the workers. The Satsuma ware is in another class.

This first-hand description gives collectors a clear explanation as to the reasons why the M-wreath, Maple leaf, and RC marked Nippon items are more desirable, artistically finished, and of a higher quality than other porcelain marked Nippon.

Baron Ichizaemon Morimura

By Rachel Altounian

Baron Ichizaemon Morimura, a true entrepreneur who possessed all the ingredients for successful trade relations with the United States, was far from being an avaricious, self-seeking businessman. When you consider that he was the product of a civilization that closed its doors to outsiders for 200 years, you could really call him a pioneer. His common sense philosophy combined with foresight in business made him a leader among Japanese entrepreneurs of the late nineteenth and early twentieth centuries.

The *Japan Year Book* of 1919 included the following under their who's who listing:

Morimura, Ichizaemon, Baron. Banker and exporter, born October 1839 in Tokyo, worked his way from obscurity to attain his present eminence in business circles, having been engaged in export and import business for two decades and more, maintaining branch stores in New York and other places, runs the Morimura Bank and was once director of the Bank of Japan. Address: Takanawa, Shita, Tokyo.

Morimura's beginnings are outlined by Johannes Hirchener in his book, *The Origins of Entrepeneurship in Meiji Japan*:

Morimura, Ichizaemon is probably the most interesting among these trade merchants because of his extraordinary idealism. At the age of 13 he had vowed before a shrine never to deviate from the path of honesty, and he not only kept his promise faithfully but became a fighter for high business ethics. He started in great poverty, running a night stall in Tokyo. Gradually Morimura gained some ground, tried his luck in mining operations, then in fishing and salt production, and profited from government trade commissions. But, surprisingly, he severed his ties as an official merchant because of the corruption that prevailed in these commission deals. He then turned to foreign trade; he had his younger brother learn English and sent him to New York for further study; this brother opened a branch office of Morimura in New York. Morimura was extremely conscious of being different from most of the other merchants in his stress for absolute honesty. He eventually extended his activities to banking and cotton spinning; he also built several schools.

In 1892, Morimura donated 1,000 yen to Japan's first laboratory for infectious diseases. He also gave to a private sanitarium for tubercular patients. In 1898 he established the Morimura Bank in Tokyo. He also contributed to the establishment of the Japan Women's University.

In *Capitalism and Nationalism in Prewar Japan* by Byron K. Marshall, Morimura is praised and quoted:

It was the "objective" view that was stressed most often by businessmen in discussing their own motivations and careers. In his rejection of individualism, Ichizaemon Morimura, made a baron for his part in the development of trade with the United States, emphasized the interdependence of men in society. He claimed that he had always felt that his first duty as a businessman was 'to act in such a way as to express gratitude for the benefits he had received from society. The secret to success in business is the determination to work for the sake of society and mankind as well as for the future of the nation, even if it means sacrificing oneself!'

Morimura was a charter member of the Japanese American Relations Committee, established in 1916. In Article One of its constitution, the aim of the organization is stated "to bring about a better understanding between the people of Japan and the people of the United States of America in order that friendly relations between them may permanently be maintained; and also to take such measures as necessary to solve any difficulty which may rise between them at any time." The membership of the committee did not exceed 30.

Apart from his philosophy, Morimura's success resulted from his surmounting the two main causes of the slow growth of Japan's foreign trade. One, the products and manufacturers of Japan were not sufficiently advertised abroad; and second, few Japanese merchants traded directly with foreign countries, preferring to conduct commercial transactions through the medium of the foreign commission houses in the several treaty-ports. Because of his direct trade to the United States and the marketing and sales strategy of his wares from his New York branch, Morimura was ahead of his competition. Thus, a strong foundation was formed, leading to the acquisition of future companies which still exist today.

The Evolution of Nippon from Victorian Times to Art Deco

By Ed and Joan Vanzo

Perhaps the most outstanding characteristic of Nippon is its vast diversity in both form and decoration. It is not unusual for Nippon dealers with many years of experience to remark that they have never seen a given piece before. In the five books of this series there is shown an enormous array of pieces with different shapes and ornamentation. In this chapter we will examine some of the factors contributing to this variety.

Although Nippon was made in Japan, the shapes and decorations were made to appeal to the tastes of customers in the country to which the merchandise was exported. This is pointedly demonstrated by the use of the scene, "The Hunter," by N. C. Wyeth on several Nippon pieces. This scene of an Indian holding a bow and a goose slung over his back was a popular print, and its reproduction on porcelain articles undoubtedly helped in obtaining orders. It is apparent that the salespeople sent samples and/or designs to Japan where they were copied.

The forms and decorations popular in the United States were to a large extent imported from Europe. Although many people had left their homelands to start a new life, they were still heavily influenced by the fashion trends overseas. The Nippon period, from 1891 to 1921, was a time of major changes in both the fashion world and the industrial world.

The end of the nineteenth century saw the close of the Victorian era, which encompassed many variations in styles but is commonly associated with heavy, ornate decoration. Although Nippon had a small market share in the 1890 – 1900 period, there still survives a good number of pieces in the "Victorian" style. In the late 1880s the beginning of a new style, Art Nouveau, was introduced in Europe and in the last decade of the nineteenth century grew in popularity. This style, characterized by sinuous lines, affected both the shape and decoration of objects. Art Nouveau reached the height of its popularity around the turn of the century.

The Modern Movement, which reflected the desire of manufacturers to simplify designs to enable mass production, began at the Paris International Exhibition in 1900. Modernism concentrated on form and was influenced by Cubism, tribal art, Egyptian art, and industrial design. The style, designed to be new, dynamic, and functional, was eventually called "Art Deco" after the Exposition des Arts Decoratifs et Industriels Modernes in Paris in 1925.

There was no sharp demarcation of the time period during which the various styles were popular, and undoubtedly there was much overlapping when one style was losing popularity and being replaced by another. We can represent the various influences by a chart showing a bell-shaped curve denoting the beginnings, height of popularity, and gradual demise of the style as follows:

To examine the influence of the different styles, we need to examine Nippon porcelain pieces that can be attributed to that specific era. It is unfortunate that Nippon was not dated in a fashion similar to the English Registry marks or a Rookwood type scheme; however, despite the loss of records during World War II, we are fortunate to know the time periods during which many of the marks were used. According to the Noritake Company:

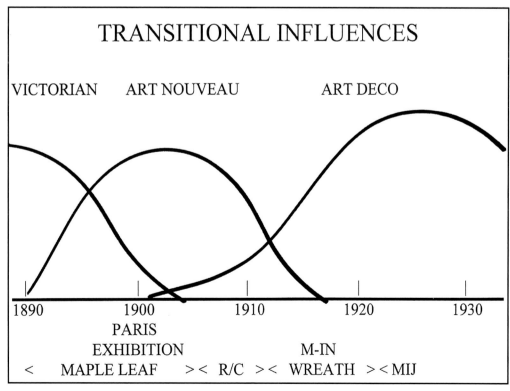

TRANSITIONAL INFLUENCES

VICTORIAN   ART NOUVEAU   ART DECO

1890   1900   1910   1920   1930

PARIS
EXHIBITION   M-IN
< MAPLE LEAF   > < R/C > < WREATH > < MIJ

Maple leaf	First used by Morimura Bros. in 1891
RC Nippon	Made for export to the United States beginning 1906
M-in-wreath	Registered for the U.S. market in 1911

We can surmise: 1. Maple leaf marked items were made in the early years no later than 1911 and possibly before 1906; 2. RC marked Nippon was made after 1906; and 3. M-in-wreath marked Nippon was made after 1911. In addition, the back stamp, "Noritake M-in-wreath Made in Japan," was used after 1918. This information gives us four points of reference to place pieces in relative time slots.

In order to demonstrate the stylistic influences, it is appropriate to examine examples that were made for some uniform purpose throughout the Nippon era. In this context, the condensed milk jar is ideal. After the invention of condensed milk in 1856 and the advent of canned condensed milk, many different containers for the storing of condensed milk cans were used until the introduction of household refrigerators in the 1920s. Containers were made of pottery, glass, silver plate, and porcelain. Twelve examples are described below and pictured on pages 15 – 17. By far the most common found today are of the porcelain variety.

Figure 1. A classical Victorian piece, this piece bears the maple leaf mark. Notice the total decoration of the piece with gaudy design utilizing a good deal of gold and flower medallions. Although the Victorian era encompasses a wide variety of styles, the heavily decorated porcelains were typical of the late nineteenth century.

Figure 2. Although the same form and mark as the previous example, this piece shows a significant amount of undercoated space, and the decoration includes a few of the looping, sinuous lines associated with Art Nouveau. This may be considered a transitional piece bridging the gap between Victorian and Art Nouveau.

Figure 3. Still a maple leaf mark, this piece exhibits the sinuous lines of Art Nouveau in both mold design and decoration. From the bulged lid and body to the curved handles and underplate this piece exudes Art Nouveau.

Figure 4. Although still a maple leaf mark and still strongly Art Nouveau with its pastel colors and naturalistic decoration, this piece demonstrates geometrical influence with angular handles and hexagonal cover and underplate.

Figure 5. This piece has the same form as Figure 4; however, the decoration is a stylized motif, more of an Art Deco flavor. The mark is RC Nippon, indicating a post 1906 origin, possibly closer to 1910. Art Nouveau

was pretty much over, and the beginnings of Art Deco were starting to influence design as well as form.

Figure 6. Again the same geometric form, the design of this piece shows more linear rather than curving elements in the decoration. This piece exhibits the "Green M-in-wreath" mark, indicating an origin after 1911.

Figure 7. A drastic change in form with straight simple lines and handles makes this mold much easier to mass produce. The decoration is more limited although it still retains a naturalistic flower and leaf design, a carry-over of the Art Nouveau influence. This piece was likely produced early in the 1911 to 1921 time span of the "Green M-in-wreath" era.

Figure 8. The same mark and form of the previous piece, this example incorporates the use of "stylized" leaves and flowers. The diaper pattern still reflects the Art Nouveau taste.

Figure 9. This piece has the same mark and shape as the previous example with a similar decoration; however, the Art Nouveau features have largely disappeared in favor of a geometrical treatment.

Figure 10. In this example with the same mark, a more classical Art Deco treatment of the decoration is evident with very stylized "flowers" and heavy geometrical content.

Figure 11. An even greater simplification of the handle design would undoubtedly make this mold more economical to mass produce. The flowers have a very abstract design, typical of Art Deco pieces. Although still a "Green M-in-wreath" mark, this piece was probably made very much toward the end of the Nippon era when Art Deco was in full swing.

Figure 12. This piece has the Noritake "Green M-in-wreath Made in Japan" mark, which dates it after 1918. The handles were omitted and the finial simplified for greater ease of production. The design is classical Art Deco; therefore it more likely was manufactured in the 1920s during the peak of Art Deco popularity.

With these examples of condensed milk jars, we have illustrated the influence of a few popular styles and the increasing pressure of mass production on shape and decoration. The Nippon era began at the end of the Victorian period, gaining market share as the Victorian style gave way to the fashionable Art Nouveau with its curvy, sinuous lines and finally ending as the wild geometric patterns and bright colors of Art Deco were reaching the height of popularity. There were other factors which were reflected in Nippon decoration, including popular scenes, prints, etc. At the very least, with an understanding of the changes in popular styles and the drive toward mass production, we can appreciate a little more the wide variety of Nippon that is our pleasure to collect.

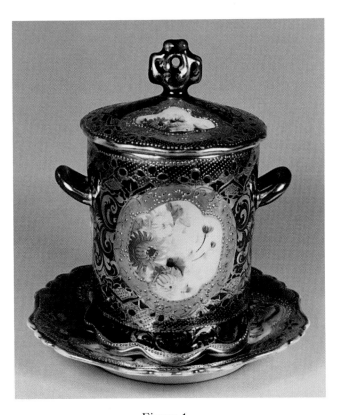

Figure 1.

Figure 2.

Figure 3.

Figure 4.

Figure 5.

Figure 6.

Figure 7.

Figure 8.

Figure 9.

Figure 10.

Figure 11.

Figure 12.

The more we study our Nippon items, the more we realize how much the Japanese copied other popular wares of the time.

Collectors have discovered that several Nippon items feature Jean Francois Millet's work. "The Gleaners" was painted in 1857 and a decal featuring this painting is found on a wonderful Nippon vase. This is a very complex design and would have required much work on the part of the artist, so a medallion was designed on the item and included a decal of this work. Old Butler Bros. catalog ads from the 1907 – 1916 period show us how popular Millet's works were at this time.

Millet had a deeply rooted respect for the rural laborers and he often painted gleaners, reapers, and woodcutters. Thousands of reproductions of this famous painting have been sold over the years, I think partly due to Millet's romanticized feeling for the soil and the sad solemnities of the peasant's toil.

"The Gleaners" portrays three peasant women collecting the scanty remains of the harvest after it has been reaped. In the original painting, harvesters can be seen loading up the plentiful crop in the background. The gleaners are reduced to laboring over the slim pickings which have been left.

Regarded as one of the masterpieces of the nineteenth century, the painting has a cool, golden light which gives dignity to the figures. But it is a harsh social comment on the poor, peasant classes of that era.

References to gleaning go back as far as the days of the Old Testament. The Hebrews were instructed to provide for those in need and Israelite law demanded that farmers leave the corners of their fields unharvested, providing food for travelers and the poor. When the fields were to be harvested of wheat and barley, reapers were hired to cut down the stalks and tie them into bundles. Any grain that was dropped was to be left for the gleaners. Poor people were free to pick up this leftover grain. This law served as a type of welfare program in Israel. It provided for food not only for the poor but also for travelers and prevented the owners from hoarding.

Owners of grape crops were also instructed not to strip every last piece of fruit from the vines, and they were not to pick up the grapes that fell to the ground.

When owners of olive trees beat the olives from the trees, they were told not to go over the boughs twice but to leave something for the migrants, orphans, and widows. People were instructed to leave the remainder for those in need.

Millet (Oct. 4, 1814 – Jan. 20, 1875) was a master painter, a peasant's son born in Normandy, France. He first studied with a Cherbourg artist, Langloisde Chevreville, and demonstrated early artistic ability. Soon after, he entered the study of Paul Dalaroche and was a close friend of Theodor Rousseau. He retired to the countryside around Barbizon and devoted himself to the painting of peasant life upon which his fame is established. He did not picture the peasants at play but rather emotionalized the labors of the soil, no doubt due to the influences of his childhood. He painted farm laborers at work or enjoying the quiet peace of the evening. All his works depict the noble toil of the peasants.

"The Angelus" was painted in 1859. In this oil painting two peasants are in the field giving thanks for their crops. In the Roman Catholic church, Angelus means prayer to the Virgin. "The Angelus" was one of Millet's favorite paintings. It appears to be a romantic veneration of peasant life and rural simplicity painted in soft colors. The dictionary describes Angelus as a prayer said at morning, noon, and evening in the Roman Catholic church and also the bell rung to tell the time for this prayer. In "The Angelus" Millet wanted to give an impression of the church bells ringing in the background. The two peasants, a man and a woman, hear the Angelus; they rise, stop work, and standing bareheaded with eyes cast down, recite a prayer. The Nippon Angelus appears to be an adaptation of the original.

"The Sower" was painted by Millet around 1850. It has a hazy atmosphere and depicts a man with a grain bag filled with seed on his left arm. He is wearing a shirt and breeches and is throwing grain in the furrows as he walks along. Millet made several drawings and pastels of "The Sower" and I believe the one depicted on several of our Nippon items is an adaptation of this famous work of art. Ours is sometimes referred to as Johnny Appleseed. It is slightly different from the original but close enough to assume that it may have been copied.

The Angelus.

The Gleaners.

16

THE SOWER.

From the 1881 book *Jean Francois Millet* by Albert Sensior.

IMPORTED WALL PLAQUE.

Appropriate for Dutch dining rooms, halls, etc.

P2513—11¾ in. diam., full size Asti heads, Angelus, Gleaners, Juvenile and foreign landscape subjects, ¾ in. beaded gilt outer edge. 1 doz. box, asstd. Doz. **95c**

Ad from Fall/Winter 1916 Butler Bros. catalog.

"ART" OFFERING

TABLE PLATE.

Specially attractive holiday seller.

R2442—9¾ in., picture center in colors and enamel of the "Gleaners" and "Angelus," chocolate shaded ground, outer gold frame, rich dark green flange with gold floral wreath, gold edge. 1 in pkg.

Each. **75c**

Ad from Dec. 1908 Butler Bros. catalog.

FRAMED MEDALLION.

Famous "Gleaners" and "The Angelus," by Jean Francois Millet. Crackerjack $2.00 leaders.

P232—16x20, 2½ in. new design prepared frame, circassian walnut finish, gold center lining, reproductions in original color of Millet's 2 masterpieces mounted on glass with wide olive green border, double gold line decorated, fancy corners. 1 in box...Each, **$1.25**

Ad from Fall 1907 Butler Bros. catalog.

Gleaners Vase, 11½" tall, green mark #47.

Close-up of Gleaners vase.

The Angelus vase, 9¼" tall, green mark #47.

The Angelus vase, 11½" tall, green mark #47.

The Sower wall plaque.

Copying Audubon

The wonderful Nippon relief molded (blown-out) eagle wall plaque shown in Plate 1470 appears to be an adaptation of one of John James Audubon's bird paintings.

Audubon was a gifted artist who dedicated his life to the work he loved. His love of nature has been traced to his early years. He began studying birds in his own backyard while still a young boy. In 1820 he gave up his business career to dedicate his life to painting all the known birds in North America. He was a perfectionist who spent days and weeks hunting for specimens to study and paint.

Audubon's work, *The Birds of America*, was completed in 1838. The final product featured 435 hand-colored plates depicting 1,065 life-sized birds.

Shown are photos of the wall plaque and an old Audubon print of the eagle.

Wall plaque, 10½" wide, green mark #47.

Audubon print.

Nippon Galle Type Wares

Our so-called Galle pattern name was assigned to this design by collectors many years ago. It was thought that this pattern resembled Galle's cameo glass. Whether this was an attempt by the Noritake Company to copy these wares is not known, but the similarity is definitely there.

The technique for engraving layered or cameo glass was Galle's specialty. His pieces were constructed of several layers of glass, each of a different color. The engraver pared away, thinning each layer to create a blended intermediate range of colors. Galle's wares were symbolist or naturalistic in theme and shape.

Emille Galle (1846 – 1904) was the premier glass artist of his generation. His work is immediately recognized by collectors. His love and knowledge of botany had a big effect on his work. He had an intense interest in nature and an intimate knowledge of plant and insect life. Galle also had a passion for Japanese art — deliberate asymmetry and a daring use of silhouettes. He used the technique of pitting of tree trunks to make them look more realistic. Nippon Galle scenes have a distinctive border, green with a white beaded edging. The fall-like shades of oranges, browns, and greens are featured. Nippon collectors find these wares very desirable and are always happy to add a piece or two to their collection.

Galle style vase.

Galle style wall plaque.

Noritake Company Salesman Pages

In this series I have included many copies of original salesman pages of the Noritake Company (pages 25 – 32). A number of them are stamped "Not for Sale, Salesman Use, Made in Japan." It's difficult to believe that salesmen used these wonderful drawings and paintings to show their customers what was available and many show the actual order written right on the paper!

Several of the pages are from the archives of the Noritake Company and were obtained through the help of Osamu (Sam) Tsutsui. The remainder are from the collection of Dr. Dennis and Susan Buonafede. They have managed to amass some wonderful salesman pages, including ones featuring portraits and cobalt items! These pages link us with our past and the items we love to collect.

Since all hand-painted work differs slightly, we can only assume that the finished items were somewhat different than the prototypes. Very often we find interpretations of designs from the decorator's own sketches. There are color variations, an extra bud added to a floral piece, etc. The amount of time spent and the individual skill of the artist also played a part in what the finished item would look like.

We can also see how a particular pattern evolved over the years by comparing the 1922 salesman page (from my collection) with the actual items found in this pattern. A photo of earlier Nippon era wares is also shown for comparison.

1922 salesman page (right) and matching items, top left and right.

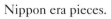
Nippon era pieces.

201
139/204/5

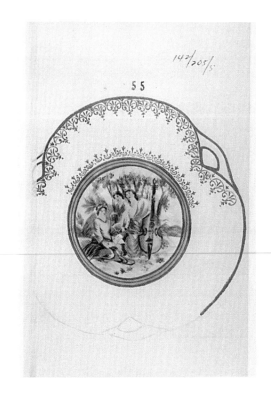

142/205/5

55

B
421

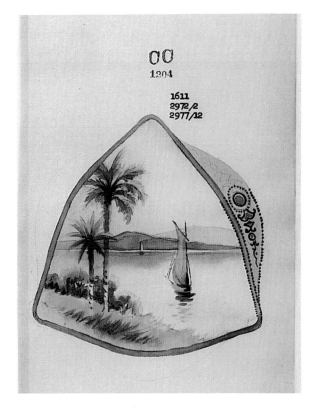

OO
1304

1611
2972/2
2977/12

A
422

326
327
1335

B 403

#644

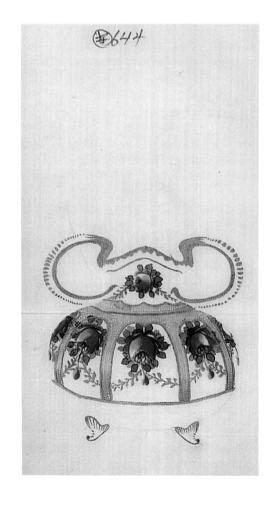

E X A
126

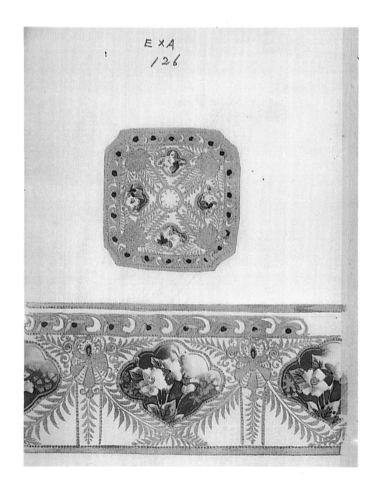

A
866

217
256
411
1708

B
896

1330

4 17

SA
1094   2616/2

B
563

458
700
737
1034
1397

B ~~578~~
678   1154

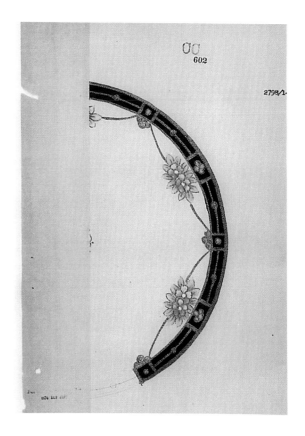

OO
602

2798/1-

OO
447
1609

B
1171
739

BB
420

1443/2
1446/2
2667/6
2664/1.3.
2668/2

D
816

545
1575

The Jewel Tea Company Connection

Nippon era items were both inexpensive and plentiful. They could be found in the five and dimes, department stores, and souvenir shops, anywhere and everywhere. And recently I discovered that they were also given as premiums by the Jewel Tea Company.

As a little girl I can remember seeing the Jewel Tea man drive up and down our rural highway and, of course, he stopped every two weeks or so at my grandmother's house. She bought vanilla and other baking supplies from him as well as obtaining pieces of the Autumn Leaf Hall china. For years I thought that was the only premium the Jewel Tea Company offered. But, lo and behold, much to my surprise and delight, I discovered that Nippon items were offered as premiums during the early years. One glance at the old ads in the booklet "Jewel Ways" and collectors will immediately recognize the chocolate sets, vases, lemonade sets, berry sets, sweetmeat sets — the list goes on and on. Three special ladies helped me in my hunt — Gwynneth Harrison, Harriet Kurshadt, and Catherine Otto. Gwynn got me started and led me to the others.

Catherine wrote to me telling of the "special" vase she had passed down to her. Her grandmother resided in South Baltimore, Md., in the early 1900s, and from the time Catherine was a little girl, she knew the story of the vase. Her grandmother had received it as a premium for buying Jewel Tea products. She, too, can remember the Jewel Tea man coming every week or so in a truck marked with the Jewel Tea logo.

Her grandmother and mother would buy vanilla, tea, assorted spices, and other food items. When her grandmother died in the early '40s, her mother inherited the vase. When Catherine's mother died, it became hers. She says it means the world to her because it has remained in the family for so many years.

Because Catherine remembers the circumstances so vividly, we now know for certain that this particular piece is one of the premiums of the Jewel Tea Company and bore the backstamp shown below.

Gwynn has located two lemonade cups that look like those featured in one of the old ads. The mark is our China E-Oh backstamp. She wonders if it could be a logo for the Jewel Tea Company. The letters JT were incorporated in some of their other backstamps, so perhaps she's right. Maybe further research will give us the answer.

Front view.

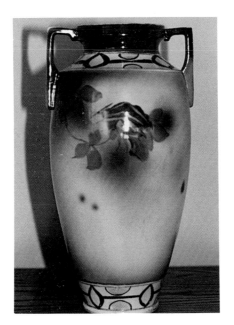

Back view.

Most items bearing the China E-Oh backstamp are not of the same fine quality as our Noritake Company wares, but that is probably to be expected since they were premiums given by the Jewel Tea Company. The sweetmeat set shown below is typical of these premiums. The case is 12" across and each crescent dish measures 5½" across. Only the center dish is backstamped.

Jewel Tea Company Family

By Harriett Kurschadt

Harriett Kurshadt is a Jewel/Autumn Leaf consultant and worked for the Jewel Tea Company for 37 years. She has copies of "Jewel Ways," a house publication directed to Jewel salesmen dated from the 1916 – 19 period. She was kind enough to give readers the following information as well as sharing the old ads.

I was asked to write something about the Jewel Tea Company and the companies that became part of it. In looking through my archives I found it a fascinating subject with some discrepancies about the early beginnings.

I am going to try and list every Jewel company (and there are a lot of them). However, the emphasis will focus on the old Jewel Tea Company in which collectors have the most interest.

You'll find little in the way of sales facts and figures…that's another story. But, I will include the things you might find interesting.

1899 – 1981 — The Jewel Tea Company

Tradition has it that Frank Skiff, a young man from Newton, Iowa, worked for about a year (1898) for the India Tea Company. He became disgruntled, and in 1899 with $700 capital, a horse, and a used wagon, founded his own company. (An old house organ, "The Tattler" of June 7, 1940, gives the date of June 7, 1899 as the official starting day.)

Business was okay, and his brother-in-law, Frank Ross, joined him as a partner. Here's the discrepancy, about half my sources said that Ross became a partner in 1900, the other half, 1901.

At any rate, they got another horse and wagon, rented a store at 643 E. 43rd Street in Chicago, and began the Jewel Tea Company, Skiff & Ross, Proprietors. According to Verna Ross Orndorff, Frank's daughter, roses were presented to the ladies who visited on the first day. (Another source says the store was opened in 1901.)

The partners called the new company "Jewel Tea" even though coffee was the chief sales item. The choice of the name "Jewel" was indicative of the times, as anything thought superior was called a "jewel."

The success of the first year in the partnership was due in large measure to Ross's talent for turning adversity into good fortune.

When a housewife slammed a door in his face because she was annoyed by the premium "come on", Ross returned and offered her a premium in advance (six Haviland china plates) provided she would buy future products from him. This would enable her to save the necessary premium coupons (one version shown at right) required to purchase the complete set.

Thus, the housewife was trusted with the use of the premium during her earning period, a revolutionary idea at the time. Haviland china was a much coveted premium, beyond the financial resources of most families. The housewife agreed, and the first order under the new "premium advancement policy" was executed.

It was to be said many years later, by sophisticated marketing experts, that this policy set the company apart and contributed substantially to its early success.

Premium coupon.

Giving out premium coupons was discontinued in 1914 in favor of the salesman keeping track of his customer's "premium balance" in his route/record book.

1904 — Company was incorporated under the name Jewel Tea Company. Additional routes were established outside of Chicago in the Illinois/Indiana area until there was a total of 12 routes in operation.

1905 — A building was leased at Randolph & May in Chicago and the first roasting of their own coffee was begun. Sales totaled $250,000.

1906 — Manufacturing under their own brand label was started; the first product was baking powder.

1908 — Coffee sales were so good that a 42-car train was required to bring this biggest shipment to one company to Chicago. A postcard of this train can be found.,

1909 — A new Chicago manufacturing plant was built at Washington Boulevard and Ada Street, owned outright by the company.

1916 — The company was incorporated under the laws of the State of New York. A January 26, 1916 document reported that there were 2,425 employees. (Jewel was also building a coffee warehouse and roasting plant on the waterfront in Hoboken, N.J.)

1917 — Jewel added the first Model T trucks.

1918 — The U.S. government commandeered the Hoboken plant and wartime conditions caused Jewel's good fortunes to begin to slump.

1919 – 1920 — Frank Skiff was forced to leave the business, and the company faced some hard, hard times.

1922 — John Hancock was elected to the office of president. With his leadership, the company made the turnaround and had profitable sales results each year until its demise in 1981.

1923 — "Jewel News," a publication for customers was begun, with a column by "The Jewel Lady."

1926 — In January, the Jewel Lady got a new name, "Mary Dunbar," the maiden name of the lady who was hired to lead this new endeavor, Mary Reed Hartson.

First store circa 1900.

business was effected. The last horse and wagon was sold.

1927 — Leone Rutledge Carroll was hired to be Mary Dunbar. She was employed for 17 years and was Jewel's first female executive.

1930 — Jewel Tea Company, Inc. moved to its new home in Barrington, Ill., a five-story building with offices on the fifth floor, and manufacturing and warehousing facilities. This building was very modern in providing employee benefits — a 4-lane bowling alley and a handball court in the basement, tennis courts, and a softball field outside. (No longer in use as such.)

1931 — The Home Service Division was renamed — now "Jewel Homemaker's Institute."

1932 — Jewel Food Stores acquired.

1933 — Autumn Leaf Hall china introduced

1943 — It is World War II time and Jewel becomes instrumental in developing 10-in-One K rations for the military (a collectible may be found).

1966 — Company name changes to Jewel Companies, Incorporated with a corporate staff for the umbrella company, and separate corporate structures from president on down for each of the many other Jewel Companies. Our Jewel becomes known as the Direct Marketing Division, or the Jewel Home Shopping Service.

1967 – 1980 — Not much noteworthy in this time span that affects the Home Shopping Service that would interest collectors, except that Jewel & Hall China cease manufacturing and selling to its route customers.

1981 — Jewel Home Shopping Service is no more. Jewel Companies, Inc. discontinues ownership, and writes off $7.5 million in assets to keep the new cooperative (the former Jewel Tea), IHSS, Inc. as it is now known, solvent.

1989 — The bank (Northern Trust of Chicago) forecloses and J.T.'S assets are sold to J. T. Merchandise Services, Inc., a wholly owned subsidiary of Furst McNess of Freeport, Illinois on July 19, 1986. Selling price: $1.4 million. As with every new company, things get changed, but the basic salesman-customer relationship remains virtually the same. The name on the truck still says "J.T.'s General Store" but the logo design changes.

1994 (October 3) — The company changes hands again. The name on the truck remains the same (with a logo design change) and the new company is called JT Dealer Sales and Services Corp. The new owners are a group of executives within the company. My thanks to Dave Lussier, for the history since 1989.

This ends the narrative of the old "Jewel Tea" part of the story. There is more to tell, but it would then become a small book.

From "Sharing," a publication for the People of Jewel Companies, Inc.

⟨ JEWEL WAYS ⟩ 9

Place These Articles of Specified Merchandise in Every Home

No. 1225.   Price..$2.50.
The attractive Oriental decorations make these Chocolate Sets highly desirable for Jewel customers. White body and gold border.

No. 617.   Price...$2.50.
A Chocolate Set is always in demand and this one in particular. It is decorated with Oriental figures in native costumes on a white background

No. 761.   Price...$2.50.
The floral design on a white body is much sought after by admirers of hand painted china. We have a limited number of these Coffee Sets.

No. 1850.   Price..$2.50.
Here is the ever wanted Pansy design on the popular white body of the Coffee Set. The pretty shape of the cups is also attractive.

No. 7221.   Price..$2.50.
Because the artists painted Violets and other flowers in profusion, some salesmen have placed dozens of these Coffee Sets among their customers.

No. 1852.   Price..$2.25.
Once more are red and pink roses used with telling effect on these popular Chocolate Sets. The border is Blue and Gold.

1916 – 1917 "Jewel Ways."

8 ⟨ JEWEL WAYS ⟩

Take Advantage of the Scarcity of China in the United States

No. 1836.   Price..$2.50.
This handsome Forget-Me-Not pattern Table Set is a popular one. The background is white and the handles are traced with gold.

No. 7221.   Price..$2.50.
Just a few of this desirable pattern of Table Sets. Dainty floral designs of various colors on white background. Gold tracing on handles.

No. 1835.   Price..$2.50.
This beautiful hand painted Table Set has floral decorations on a white body. The handles are gilded. A violet design is pictured.

No. 761.   Price...$2.50.
This seven-piece Imported China Lemonade Set is equally desirable for Ice Tea and Acoola. The body is white with floral decorations, such as Violets, etc.

No. 617.   Price...$2.50.
Only a limited number of these Popular Lemonade Sets this year. This one has a white body and is decorated with Oriental figures in native costumes.

No. 16–9.   Price..$2.25.
A very desirable Lemonade Set, having an amber colored body with attractive landscape decorations. Quantity limited.

1916 – 1917 "Jewel Ways."

No. 357.
Price........$2.50

This 16-inch hand painted vase with pink rose design on greenish-tan background makes a very attractive ornament for the living room.

No. 433.
Price........$2.50

This is a handsome 16-inch hand-painted vase with richly colored Japanese figures, that ought to be very popular with all who have a taste for the oriental.

1916 – 1917 "Jewel Ways."

10

❦ JEWEL WAYS ❧

Advance Your Customers THIS IMPORTED Hand-Painted China

No. 1730. Price..$2.50.
At this time of the year, our salesmen place thousands of these beautiful Berry Sets. This one shows hand painted water-lilies on a white background, with tracings of gold.

No. 1852. Price..$2.00.
Our stock of Berry Sets as pictured above is now at its best. But red and pink roses of such dainty appearance are popular.

No. 2160. Sweet Meat Sets.
Red Case — Landscape Design.
No. 2161. Green case—Bird and flower design. **Price.........$3.00**
Sweet Meat Sets are always desirable as presents.

No. 1206. Price..$2.00.
This Berry Set is also used for Ice Cream. It has an artistic floral design on a white body. The border is of gold. Only a few remaining.

No. 1225. Price..$2.50.
For those who desire a genuine Oriental pattern on a Berry Set, the above is recommended. The body is white with tracings of gold.

1916 – 1917 "Jewel Ways."

No. 1730 — Price $2.75
Water lillies in profusion decorate this Popular Lemonade Set of 7 Pieces.

THOUSANDS of pieces of imported china have been distributed throughout the entire Jewel System during the past three weeks.

Customers are only too eager to have these handsome articles of specified merchandise presented to them, many never before having had the opportunity to acquire such longed-for things.

Tell your patrons how fortunate you are in being able to deliver these articles inasmuch as very few stores in the country are able to obtain them at any price. Assure them that it is all genuine, hand painted china, imported especially for this company.

JEWEL TEA CO., Inc.

1916 – 1917 "Jewel Ways."

1917 Merchandise Price List.

JAPANESE CHINA

We carry a complete line of Fancy Japanese China, including the following items: Vases, Chocolate Sets, Lemonade Sets, Dresser Sets, Cake Sets, Berry Sets, Coffee Sets, Table Sets, Cups and Saucers, Sugars, Creamer and Tea Pot Sets, Cracker Sets, Fancy Plates, Salads, Bon Bon Dishes, Chop Plates, Fern Dishes, Tankards and Sweet Meat Sets.

A Unique Christmas Gift
Hand-Painted Sweet-Meat Sets Imported Direct From Japan For Holiday Trade

THE coming holidays promise to be most profitable for Jewel salesmen owing to the high cost of living. The housewife will be unusually chary with her Christmas money this year and will welcome the salesman who will advance her merchandise the Jewel way, according to the well known profit sharing plan of the Jewel Tea Co., Inc.

One of the newest and most attractive novelties offered this season is the beautiful "sweet-meat" set pictured on this page. The article had its origin in France where it was called "hors d'oeuvre" and is generally used in that country and in England. In Germany the set is called "kalter aufschnitt" and is found in nearly every household.

at once seen because no two dishes are exactly the same as would be the case were the designs put on by modern process. A variety of designs and colors will be found in the sweet-meat sets.

These sets were primarily intended for use in serving pickles, olives, radishes and other condiments, but today are more generally used for other purposes. They are especially desirable for the serving of shelled nuts, candied confections, bon-bons, etc. The dishes may be used for serving the confections individually if desired, or the set may be used as a community server. The empty dish will prove a very attractive coaster for serving soft drinks, etc.

1918 – 1919 "Jewel Ways."

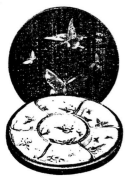

The containers are twelve inches in diameter and are made of the very best quality papier mache, which is lacquered to a high finish by a secret process in possession of the Japanese. They will positively not crack or peel, even when subjected to extreme climatic conditions. The dishes consisting of one center piece and six side dishes, are of high grade china and are hand-painted to match the hand-painted design on the cover. This is

New Jap Ware

Cups and saucers of Jap ware in a green line trimming have been added to the Jewel specified merchandise line. The tableware is heavy and substantial. At the same time it is highly attractive. You'll find this ware appeals to the average housewife strongly.

Large stocks of this ware are at Newark and Chicago. Your requisition for this specified merchandise will be honored promptly. You'll find it a great aid in placing and holding orders. The cups and saucers sell for 40 cents profit sharing credit.

Order by number N 257.

Jewel Tea Co., Inc.

1918 – 1919 "Jewel Ways."

Advancing Japanese China To Hundreds of Jewel Customers

Largest Stock of Hand Painted China from Land of Cherry Blossom Carried by Any Firm in the United States at Disposal of Jewel Patrons

Just in the very midst of the great Campaign for New Customers that is being conducted by Jewel salesmen all over the country comes the information that the great premium warehouse of the Jewel Tea Company is filled with thousands of the prettiest, daintiest, most attractive articles of Japanese chinaware that have ever been offered by this firm.

It is doubtful if more attractive gifts could be selected than the berry sets, table sets, chocolate sets, vases and lemonade sets that are pictured in this issue of "Jewel Ways." In order that the salesmen may become more familiar with this class of useful articles, Mr. C. G. Entzminger, advertising manager for one of the largest Japanese importers, was induced to tell about Japanese china. He has been identified for some years with the importation of Japanese goods and his words may be taken as authoritative regarding these products from the land of cherry blossoms.

Brief History of Japanese China

From the time of Commodore Perry's visit to Japan in 1853 until the year 1893, the importation of Japanese goods was confined largely to art objects and antiques, which were pur-

Lemonade set No. 16-9 consisting of pitcher and six mugs

chased exclusively by the wealthier classes. The Japanese exhibition at the Chicago World's Fair gave an impetus to the American demand for Oriental products which has increased

Chocolate set No. 761 consisting of seven pieces

to such proportions that now there is scarcely a home in the United States, no matter how humble, which does not exhibit some product of Japan. For many years the china which came from Japan was decorated in typical Oriental fashion and was easily distinguished as being of Japanese manufacture. The Japanese potters, however, were alert and soon adapted themselves to the American ideas of decoration, which has resulted in ceramic productions which, from a decorative standpoint, are difficult to distinguish from domestic hand painted or European retouched productions. The typical Japanese decorations, however, have not been entirely supplanted by the more modern adornments, because there is still a considerable demand for the quaint Oriental designs.

Genuineness of Japanese China

A prevalent belief regarding Japanese chinaware and porcelain is that many of the products of the Flowery Kingdom are not genuine Oriental productions, but manufactured in this country. A moment's serious thought will dispel this illusion, for the very simple reason that on account of the cheapness of Oriental labor, an imitation produced in this country would cost more than the original made in Japan. Many years' experience in the manufacture of chinaware has enabled the Japanese potters to become exceptionally proficient in this art, the consequence of which has

been a much larger output per worker than our American potters.

Cost of Japanese China

The actual time required by a Japanese artist to decorate a cup and saucer in an average floral decoration is from twenty to thirty minutes, while an American artist executing a similar piece of work would consume at least two hours. The approximate ratio of labor costs between the Japanese and American worker in the pottery industries is from one to three to one to six. In other words, while an American artist might command $6.00 per day, the Japanese artist receives about $1.00 per day. The manual laborers engaged in the pottery industries in Japan receive approximately 50c per day, while the same class of laborers in our country command about $3.00 per day. The ratio of production between the Japanese and the American artists is about four to one. In other words, the Japanese

Berry set consisting of seven pieces No. 1206

artist could decorate four cups and saucers while an American artist was decorating one. With these proportions in mind, it is very easy to understand why the price of Japanese goods is so moderate in this country, despite an import duty of 55 per cent.

American Potteries Do Not Make China

Even if the American pottery manufacturers desired to imitate the Japanese chinaware, it would be impossible for them to do so, for the reason that there is practically no chinaware manufactured in this country. The production of our domestic potteries is confined almost exclusively to the manufacture of porcelain ware, which is quite different in composition from chinaware. The ingredients which enter into the manufacture of chinaware are unlike those used in making porcelain, as a comparison of

Continued On Page Eleven

1918 – 1919 "Jewel Ways."

ADVANCING JAPANESE CHINA

Continued From Page Six

the two finished products will reveal. Chinaware is translucent; in other words, when held to the light, objects can be seen in outline through it, while porcelain is opaque and does not diffuse light.

Proof of Hand Painting

Many people do not believe that Japanese chinaware, which is stamped "Hand Painted," is actually decorated by hand. A very simple demonstration will convince the most skeptical that their conviction is wrong. As an illustration, take a Japanese water set. Select any two mugs from the set and compare them very closely. You will instantly discover that the decorations are not exactly alike. Notice the different shades in colorings on like flowers of each mug; one is darker than the other, or shows a heavier impression of the artist's brush. Compare like leaves on each of the mugs and you will observe that they are not identical in shape or color, and that the relative positions to the flow-

One of a large variety of handsome vases

ers are not the same. If the decoration is one which has gold line tracing or a conventional touch, you can easily mark the irregularity of the lines. If the decoration has a colored

background, the variations in color tones is plainly discernible. This same demonstration can be applied to all Japanese chinaware sets which are stamped "Hand Painted." Single pieces, such as vases, cake plates, salad bowls, etc., when closely examined, will reveal the trace of the artist's brush, and the absence of symmetry in the decorations proves conclusively that it is hand work.

Comparison of Hand Work and Decalcomanias

If the decorations were prints or decalcomanias, which is the decorative process employed in the manufacture of the inexpensive lines of domestic pottery and European chinaware, the result on each piece would be identical. A decalcomania is a

Table set No. 1835 consisting of sugar and creamer, bread plate, butter dish, salt and pepper set

reproduction from an original, and consequently each impression is the same and when transferred to the objects, results in a finished product which has no distinguishing characteristics. The decalcomania process can best be likened to the little colored transfer pictures which, when moistened and applied to the hand or other objects, leaves its impression. This comparison between the Japanese hand work and the decalcomania process should not be construed as being a reflection on the latter method. Many very beautiful creations are produced by decalcomanias and when retouched by hand are difficult to distinguish from free hand work.

PLACE
JAPANESE CHINA
NOW

No. 1835 Table Set

THE Management requests every Manager, every Wagon Salesman, and every Advance Salesman to make a special effort to place Japanese China with customers during the next few weeks. There is nothing more attractive in the entire list of our Specified Merchandise. Your customers will be glad to get this China, because China of any kind is scarce in this country at present. You are particularly fortunate in being able to offer it to them.

ADVANCE
JAPANESE CHINA

No. 761 Chocolate Set

China of any description is at a premium in this country right now. Take advantage of that fact. It means money in your pocket.

No. 1206 Berry Set

JEWEL TEA CO., INC.

Frequently Asked Questions

I receive many letters each month and many of the same questions appear time and time again. In this chapter I would like to address some of them for collectors.

Is there a difference in value between items marked with a green, blue, or red M-in-wreath?

I have found that the majority of items having a red, or so-called magenta mark usually are utilitarian pieces that are not so lavishly decorated as those bearing the blue or green M-in-wreath mark — hence they do not bring as high a price nor are they as much in demand. All the M-in-wreath pieces were manufactured by the Noritake Company. Both blue and green marks indicate high quality wares.

What's the purpose of items referred to as tidies?

Hair receivers were called tidies years ago and that is still the term used in England, Australia, and New Zealand, I'm told. Tidies were used to store hair. The hair was brushed and wound around the finger and then pushed into the hole in the center of the lid. Hair accumulated in these receivers was used to make rattails to be used with one's own hair or picture making with hair flowers and jewelry.

How can I tell if an item has a decal on it or is hand-painted?

Whenever you see a pattern that is of a complex nature, it's a safe bet to assume it's a decal. Hold the item under a good light, use a magnifying glass, and if you see small dots making up the pattern, you have a decal (see photos). If you see brush strokes, then it's hand-painted. Some items make use of both techniques. Most of the portrait pieces employed decals imported from France. The Noritake Company wanted to ensure that the people displayed would look European just in case the Japanese artist had difficulty painting these features. It was also a cost-effective measure.

Close-up of decals.

Close-up of hand-painted work.

Do tea and chocolate sets always have sets of six and eight cups and saucers? I've seen them with four, five, and six.

I have hundreds of old Nippon ads and in checking them, I could only find where tea and chocolate sets were sold with six cups and saucers. It was also possible to buy pots separately, and cups and saucers were sold in half dozen and dozen size packages, so I guess you could have had a dozen cups if you wanted. Most likely the sets originally had six cups and saucers and one or two have been broken over the years. Of course, a tête-à-tête set would have had only two cups and saucers.

∴ —— ∵

Why do most moriage pieces have no backstamp?

There are many reasons why an item may not be backstamped. It could predate the 1891 law, it could have been imported with a paper label which has been worn or washed off, the mark may have been scratched off, the piece may have been part of a set or in a box where only one item was marked, or perhaps the article was exported to a country where this ruling did not apply. There are some "newer" moriage type wares but the difference in texture is readily apparent to most collectors. I doubt that any company will be reproducing these wares; it would require considerably more time and effort for them than the ones they are now manufacturing. Today, we call the slip trailed items moriage, but years ago they were evidently referred to as moriago. Some of the dragon pattern pieces even had glass eyes attached. The glass crackled when it was fired.

Ads from Butler Bros. 1907 catalog.

Most pairs of urns are identical. Is it unusual to find them where the design on one is on the left and the other where it's on the right?

These are referred to as "mirror image" urns. Evidently this style was more in vogue in Great Britain in the early 1900s than the United States. Each pair I have ever found designed like this has had a backstamp indicating a Great Britain destination. They're unusual to find in the United States.

SUGAR SHAKERS.

L2480—4x4¾, paneled trailing blossom and leaf spray, conventional band border, gold lined edges and handle, gold starred top. 1 doz. in box..........................Doz. 96c

SCREW TOP

L9421—5 in., ivory tinted, paneled, gold outlined pink lotus blossoms and green leaves beaded gold band, gold dec. top and line base. 3 in box.
EACH. 36c

Old ads from Butler Bros. catalogs.

Sugar shaker with cover.

Do all sugar shakers have a cork in the bottom?

They have either a cork in the bottom or a screw top. There are also those that have a cover; the holes in the top are concealed by it and it has a cork in the bottom. Sugar shakers are taller and wider than salt and pepper shakers.

Basket vases in different sizes.

On the bottom of some of my items I have found a raised star or long raised bar. Is this an additional mark? Does it increase the value of the item?

Both of these raised marks are called spur marks and were added to the item only to give it strength when it was fired in the kiln. It adds no value to the item although some people think it does. ·◡———◡·

I have two odd shaped vases. Neither will hold many flowers. Do you think they had another use?

Yes, decoration! One is referred to by collectors as a bottle vase and the other is a basket vase. One or two flowers would fit, but most likely they were used as cabinet pieces.

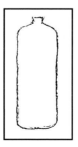

Bottle vase.

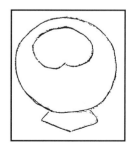

Basket vase.

Pancake warmer (notice steam holes in top).

Butter dish.

How do you tell a covered pancake server from a covered butter dish?

If you suspect that something warm was to be kept inside, check to see if it has a steam hole or two. A pancake warmer will, a butter dish will not.

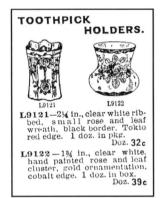

TOOTHPICK HOLDERS.

L9121   L9122

L9121—2¼ in., clear white rib-bed, small rose and leaf wreath, black border. Tokio red edge. 1 doz. in pkg.
Doz. **32c**

L9122—1¾ in., clear white, hand painted rose and leaf cluster, gold ornamentation, cobalt edge. 1 doz. in box.
Doz. **39c**

Toothpick holder.

HATPIN HOLDER

L7530—5½ in., forget-me-not decoration with spray and fancy gold trimming, gold lined edges. 1 doz. in pkg.
Doz. **96c**

Hatpin holder.

TOOTH BRUSH HOLDER.

L9123—4¼x2¼, clear white, scenic decor., green edges. 1 doz. in pkg............Doz. **75c**

Toothbrush holder.

How can I tell the difference between an open hatpin holder, a tooth-brush holder, and a toothpick holder?

An open hatpin holder is the tallest usually 5" in size, and narrower than a tooth brush holder which is about 4" tall and wider than a hatpin holder. A toothpick holder is about 2" in height. A glance at old ads will show the differences.

᭶——————᭷

What's the difference between a stein and a mug?

Height. A stein will be about 7" tall, a mug, 5" or less. Shaving mugs are about 4" tall.

᭶——————᭷

What's the difference between a chamberstick and a candlestick?

A chamberstick is usually shorter in height and has an attached plate and handle for holding the piece. Candlesticks are taller, generally 7 – 11" in height.

᭶——————᭷

SALT AND PEPPER SHAKERS.
Each with cork. 1 dz. box, 6 salts, 6 peppers.

L7032   L6181   L7743   L7165

L7032—3 in., 2 styles Japanese scene, floral border, Tokio red top and base......Doz. **32c**

L6181—3¼x2¼, allover Japanese decoration cobalt top & base, gold ornamented.
Doz. **42c**

L7743—2 styles, 3½ in., ribbed, lt. green tints, current and grape decors., shaded green foliage, gold ornamented cobalt band, gold decorated top...................Doz. **45c**

L7165—3½ in., paneled, pastel tints, cherry trees, gold line neck and base...................Doz. **69c**

L8185—3 in., hexagon, clear white china, gold outlined pink roses and leaves, beaded gold scrolls, gold decorated top and line base.
Doz. **85c**

L8185

How do you tell a stickpin holder from a salt shaker?

A stickpin holder will be about 1½" tall and most salt shakers fall in the range of 2½" to 3½" tall.

᭶——————᭷

What's a muffineer?

A muffineer is just another name for a sugar shaker.

How do you distinguish between a celery dish and a pickle or relish dish?

A celery dish will generally be 9" – 12" long whereas a relish dish will be smaller. Some of the so-called relish and pickle dishes we find today were once called spoon trays and used for spoons on the table. Many of the items had dual roles.

SPOON TRAY OR PICKLE DISH.

L2436—9¾ in., lt. tan border, gold outlined, red and lavender floral and leaf sprays with connecting stems, gold beaded edge, gold center medallion. ¼ doz. in box. .Doz. $3.60

Berry bowl and underplate.

Did all pierced berry bowls originally come with an underplate?

It only makes sense that they would have. When berries were placed in the bowl, they probably had just been rinsed with water and were wet. Without an underplate, drops of water would have been all over the table.

What do you think is the finest Nippon chinaware and which do you think is inferior quality?

When we talk of fine wares, we mean those that are translucent, have a bell-like sound when tapped, are smooth to the touch, and have the whitest and thinnest porcelain. In my opinion, those that have the best porcelain bear the RC (Royal Crockery) mark. The most ornate and generally the best decorated pieces are those bearing the maple leaf mark; the M-in-wreath mark is next. Generally pieces with the China E-oh mark and the pagoda mark were not made of the best quality porcelain. Items bearing the Royal Nishiki mark are usually of a softer paste material and do not have the fine quality of most of the other Nippon pieces. The rising sun mark is found on utilitarian pieces. The quality of the porcelain is fine but the decoration is very plain.

Were all items backstamped with Nippon made by the Noritake Company?

The words Nippon and Noritake are not synonymous. Nippon is the name of the country of origin so anything could have been backstamped with this word during the 1891 – 1921 period, musical instruments, lacquer boxes, etc. Noritake is the name of the company located in Nippon (Japan). If an item is marked Noritake that indicates that it was made by the Noritake Company in Japan, but if an item is marked Nippon, that does not necessarily mean that it was manufactured by the Noritake Company.

I want to sell some Nippon items. How do I go about pricing them and finding buyers?

Check the Nippon books for similar items to get an idea of pricing. Keep in mind that prices shown in the books are retail prices and generally not what a dealer is willing to pay. Price your items fairly and run an ad in one of the antique trade papers. Be prepared to send photos to prospective buyers and guarantee the merchandise. Always check over your pieces for chips, gold wear, etc., and describe them accurately.

What does the M in the M-in-wreath stand for? An N would make more sense as they were produced by the Noritake Company.

The M stands for Morimura (Morimura Bros. was the forerunner of the Noritake Company) and the wreath was designed from the crest of the Morimuras. Morimura Bros. of New York City was also the importer of Japanese wares to the United States from 1876 to 1941. The M-in-wreath is found under the glaze in green, blue, magenta, and gold colors. According to Noritake Company records, the letter N in the backstamp was first registered in Japan in 1953 but used as early as 1952.

When did the Noritake Company start making dinnerware sets?

Noritake Company records indicate that their first dinnerware pattern was Sedan in 1914. The registration date is unknown but the pattern number is listed as D1441. Since then the Noritake Company has manufactured more than 3000 patterns of dinnerware.

Did egg warmers ever have a cork as a stopper?

Egg warmers hold 4-6 eggs. They always came with a porcelain stopper. If one is found with a cork you can be sure this is a replacement. The stopper was lifted out of the item, hot water was poured inside, stopper was replaced, and the eggs were kept warm.

Did ferners originally come with inserts?

Old ads indicate that most did. I have found a few where a metal container was still inside the ferner. Most are found without these items. One old ad I read stated that the china fern dish came with an inside perforated removable clay pot. I have never spotted one of these and it's doubtful that clay pots would have survived over the years.

Ferner with metal insert.

JAPANESE CHINA 3 PIECE SETS.
Some with Cups and Saucers to Match.

Good transparent china, hand painted decorations. Each set comprises tea pot, covered sugar bowl and cream pitcher. Each set in pkg.

L5100—Tea pot 5x4, sugar 4½x3½, creamer 4x3, ribbed melon shape, allover Japanese figure, flower and lantern decorations, gold outlined, Tokio red edges, handles, knobs and spout ....Set. 69c

JAPANESE CHINA CHOCOLATE POTS.

L2209   L2212

L2209—Ht. 7½ in., panel shape, gold traced fancy cobalt blue edges and handles, allover gold and colored floral spray decorations. ¼ doz. in pkg............Doz. $3.95

L2212—9¼ in., allover Japanese figure, landscape and water scenes profusely gold illuminated, green band edges, maroon handle and knob gold traced. 1 in pkg.
Each, 75c

L2213—9 in., fancy shape, ribbed, cream ground, rose cluster and embossed gold decoration, deep beaded gold top border, gold decorated handle and knob. 1 in pkg.
Each, 90c

L2213

What's the difference between a chocolate pot, a teapot, and a coffee pot?

A coffee pot is tall, has a long spout and a cover; a chocolate pot, although tall in size has a short spout at the top and a cover. Teapots are shorter and squatty with a long spout and cover. Milk pitchers are generally medium in height, some have a cover and some do not.

Demitasse or after dinner coffee set.

Teapots.

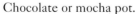

Chocolate or mocha pot.   Demitasse or after dinner coffee pot.

Sometimes you see a vase and a covered urn in the same decoration and size. When this happens, does this mean that the vase probably once had a cover?

Maybe yes and maybe no. It is possible that the cover is missing on the vase and it is also possible both type items were made bearing the same decoration. The covered urn may have a lip at the top for the cover to fit on. A covered urn should sell for more if both are in comparable condition.

What is a tête-à-tête set?

It includes a teapot, covered sugar bowl, creamer, two cups and two saucers — for more intimate talks!

.ᴗ.————.ᴗ.

What's the difference between a snack set and a refreshment set?

Nothing. Old catalogs also called these items sandwich sets, dessert sets, and toast sets. These sets consist of a plate and matching cup. The plate has an indentation on it for the bottom of the cup.

What pieces can I expect to find in a toy china tea set?

Often we find six tea plates, cups and saucers, a covered teapot, covered sugar bowl, and a cream pitcher. Most collectors think that six plates make a complete set, but I've reviewed a number of old catalog ads and they show where some were originally sold with only three or four plates, cups and saucers. So, if you find a set today with only three or four of each, it does not necessarily mean part is missing — that may be all there was originally.

.ᴗ.————.ᴗ.

What's a whip cream set?

A whip cream set consists of a small bowl, matching underplate, and a serving ladle. Collectors also call this a mayonnaise set.

.ᴗ.————.ᴗ.

What's the difference between a bouillon cup and a tea cup?

A bouillon cup will have two handles, a tea cup, only one. Many bouillon cups are found with covers.

.ᴗ.————.ᴗ.

How can I tell if an item is a wall plaque or just a rectangular tray or round plate?

Turn the item over. If it is a wall plaque there will be two or three holes on the back so wire could be threaded for hanging. Very large plaques are referred to as chargers.

.ᴗ.————.ᴗ.

When I'm out shopping, I see dealers selling humidors without covers as ferners, and sugar bowls without tops as open sugars. How does a collector know the difference?

Many of the English manufactured chinaware sugar bowls were indeed "open" sugars, but I have yet to come across a Nippon one. Old ads indicate they came with covers. The lip found around the tops of many humidors and sugar bowls is a clue to the buyer that something sat on top of these items. However, a number of Nippon humidors do not have a lip, so I suppose a novice collector could be confused. Check the Nippon books and get to know what a ferner looks like and how it differs from a humidor.

.ᴗ.————.ᴗ.

What's the difference between a syrup pitcher or an individual size teapot?

There will be a steam hole in the top of the teapot.

.ᴗ.————.ᴗ.

Is a vanity set the same as a dresser set?

Not according to old catalog ads. A vanity set is made up of two perfume bottles and a powder dish. A dresser set might include a brush, comb, tray, hatpin holder, cologne or perfume bottle, pin tray, trinket dish, stickpin holder, powder box, hair receiver, ring tree, hairpin holder and sometimes a pair of candlesticks. A manicure set was advertised with a tray, powder box, and different size jars that could be used for cold cream, powdered pumice, cuticle-ice, etc.

How do you tell the difference between a jam jar, condensed milk container, and a honey pot?

The honey pots I have found have all been in the shape of a bee-hive; the top is ribbed and decorated with bees. There's a hole in the top for a spoon or ladle which originally came with it. Jam jars and condensed milk containers look a lot alike. Both come with covers and underplates. There will be a notch in the cover of the jam jars and old ads indicate that porcelain spoons originally came with these items. A condensed milk container will have a hole in the bottom which was used to push up the can when you wanted to remove it.

CONDENSED MILK JARS.

L6477 — 3¾x5, saucer 6¼, Japanese picture decorated, Tokio red edges, handles and knob. 3 In pkg....................Each, 33c

L6478 — Ht. 5½ in., saucer 6 in., blue tinted surface, rose clusters sides and cover, gold beaded edges and ornamented handles and cover. 3 in pkg.....................Each, 39c

Jam Jar Set

No. 49010 GIVEN with a $2 purchase of Products or for $2 In Coupons.

Set consists of Jar, 3¾ in. high, Plate 6¼ in. in diameter, and Ladle. Decorated with pink, white and red roses, blended with shaded leaves. Edges are outlined in gold. Shipping weight 3 lbs.

What do you know about companies other than Noritake that produced porcelain in Japan for export during the 1891 – 1921 period?

Very little, I'm afraid. It's believed that Nagoya, which is the home of the Noritake Company, was the source of most of our porcelain. My research indicates that over 90 percent of the items we find today can be traced to the Noritake Company in Nagoya. Most records were destroyed during World War II so little is even known about the Noritake Company. In the 1930s, Nagoya's industrial growth accelerated due to its munitions and aircraft industries. This ultimately caused its ruin. American bombers virtually razed the city in WWII.

⌣———⌣

What pieces make up an oatmeal set?

An oatmeal set is made up of a bowl, small pitcher, and matching plate. It's also called a child's breakfast set by collectors.

⌣———⌣

Should collectors buy unmarked pieces of Nippon?

Absolutely, but not until they know what they are doing. There are a number of reasons why an item may not be marked, but I would suggest the beginner only buy marked pieces. Learn to identify the reproductions. They are marked Nippon but are not Nippon era wares!

⌣———⌣

How do you tell a whiskey jug from a wine jug?

As a rule of thumb, the wine jug will usually be taller and will hold more liquid. Study the different shapes shown in the books and you will see what I mean.

The whisky jugs are squattier, some are in the shape of a miniature barrel, some are bulbous, some are square, etc.; they can range in size from 5½" to 8" in height.

The wine jugs run from 7½" to 11" in height, and there are several different shapes and sizes to be found in this category.

In the interest of research, I filled several of these pieces with water. The tallest wine jug #859 holds 46 oz. and the 7¾" triangular #168 holds 44 oz. The barrel-shaped whiskey jug #1955 will only hold 22 oz. and the 7" #162 (second) holds 24 oz. So although #162 is only ¾" shorter than #168, it holds 20 oz. less. The base part that holds the majority of the liquid is always larger on the wine jugs. Some of these can still be found with their original wicker basket. And remember a wine or whiskey jug is not complete without its porcelain stopper.

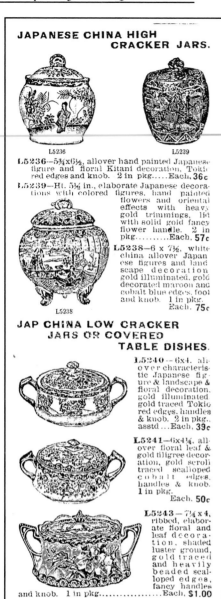

How do you tell a humidor from a cracker jar?

When you take off the cover of the humidor, you will see a hollow space in which a sponge was placed. Some are even found today with the original sponge intact.

What's the difference between a cookie jar and a cracker jar?

Collectors get accustomed to referring to items in certain ways, and the taller cookie/cracker jar is usually referred to as a cookie jar. However, old catalog ads described them as high cracker or biscuit jars and low cracker or biscuit jars and even covered table dishes. Maybe we should return to the original terminology.

What is a reticulated item?

Reticulation does not refer to a particular technique used, such as tapestry or gold overlay. It is merely a term collectors use for piercing. Holes or sections are cut in clay when it is at the leather hard stage (before it's fully dried out). An example might be a celery dish. At the edges there's a cut-out space to make handles. The potter had to be very careful when doing this as it tends to weaken the clay piece.

Holes at ends are handles.

Does color variation affect the price of an item?

It is amazing how different colors change the look of a piece! On the facing page, you see the same blown-out plaque painted in four different ways. The blue and white decor is referred to as wedgewood type — the others show the different artists' interpretations. Beauty is in the eye of the beholder, but many collectors have definite preferences which they like best and this can change the price somewhat. Good quality hand painting is always the most desirable.

Note the same dog plaque mold is painted three different ways. I have a favorite, but it just depends on which you prefer. Always buy what *you* like.

What are so-called transitional pieces?

They are what Nippon collectors believe are in-between pieces, made at the end of the Nippon era. Because the backstamp had to bear the word Japan, the mark will have both names. Both the figural flower frog and the elephant creamer and sugar bear Nippon mark #32 plus the words "Made in Japan." Figural lusterware pieces such as these do not usually bear the word Nippon in their backstamp.

Is Nippon a type of porcelain?

Nippon is merely another name for Japan, the country of origin of our porcelain items. Many types of items can be found bearing a Nippon backstamp. The pottery vase shown in the photo was made by the Noritake Company and bears a gold mark #47, green M-in-wreath backstamp. The other photos show paper Christmas lights, paper Easter eggs, a large satin type egg with painted decor, and wood and lacquer boxes with a gold and silver decor. All are stamped Nippon.

52

The following definitions are, for the most part, from a work on ceramic art by Jennie J. Young.

Pottery is from the Latin *potum*, a drinking vessel. It is applied in English usage to all opaque wares as distinguished from translucent porcelain — also to the place of manufacture. The French word *poterie*, however, is a general name for all vessels, both earthenware and porcelain.

Faience is a French word, and is applied to every kind of glazed earthenware.

Majolica is employed in very nearly the same significance. It is by some writers restricted to ware of Italian manufacture, and derived from the island of Majorca, "which lends its softened name to art."

Porcelain – signifies a vitreous and translucent ware – standing in the ranks of the fictile art much higher than pottery. The name is derived from *porcella*, a little hog; the first ware of this kind seen in Europe was the egg-shell fabric of China, to which was given the name *pourcelaine*, its translucent delicacy suggesting the beautiful univalve shell familiar to dwellers along the Mediterranean coast. The shell, in turn was called *porcella*, from its fancied resemblance in shape to the back of a pig. Porcelain is of two kinds, the natural, or pate dure, and the artificial, or pate tendre. The latter, "soft paste," was the first to be discovered in Europe by persistent chemical experiment. Evidences of the success of the potter's alchemy date back to 1580. It was not until 1709 that the accidental discovery of a bed of kaolin in Saxony led to the manufacture of hard porcelain. Two ingredients are necessary to its production: kaolin, a result of the decomposition of granite rock, and so called because found in great quantities in China, near a mountain named Kaoling; and petuntse, a pure feldspar. Kaolin is an infusible element and constitutes the body of the ware; fusible at a high temperature, petuntse envelops the kaolin and gives the translucency.

Glaze and enamel are terms often confused. Properly applied, "glaze" means a transparent covering of the ware; "enamel" is a covering which obscures the body. Silicious or glass glaze is formed by fusing sand with an alkali. The addition of oxide of lead gives transparent plumbiferous glaze. When this is combined with oxide of tin, opaque stanniferous enamel is the result. Salt glaze, the only kind of glaze produced by fumes during baking, is also used on pottery. Another is a thin, plumbeous glaze called varnish.

Bone China or English artificial porcelain is composed largely of bone in combination with kaolin and feldspar.

Parian is a composition of silica, alumina, oxide of iron, lime, magnesia, potash, and soda.

Biscuit is a technical term applied to all kinds of ware before they are enameled or glazed. It literally means twice baked, but is invariably used as a name for pottery and porcelain when but once baked.

Does an original box found with a Nippon doll or tea set add to the value of the item?

Definitely. It's the frosting on the cake in my opinion. Original stickers found on dolls also add to their value.

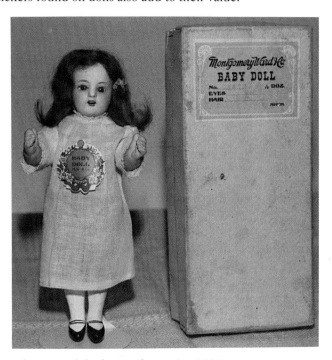

Are the porcelain items from the 1891 – 1921 period made in the same way as today's wares?

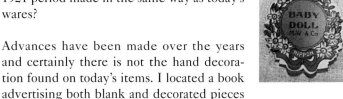

Advances have been made over the years and certainly there is not the hand decoration found on today's items. I located a book advertising both blank and decorated pieces from the early 1900s and I am sure that our Nippon articles were made in a similar fashion. (See definition box.)

᠅———᠅

Do some items have interchangeable names? Were they intended for several uses?

Going over old ads we note that jewel boxes were also called puff or powder puff boxes, also bonbon boxes or toilet boxes. Small nut dishes could also be used for salt dips, and spoon trays were the same as pickle and relish dishes; pin dishes and ashtrays were often interchanged. Chop plates and dessert plates were often the same, as well as olive, bonbon, and nut bowls.

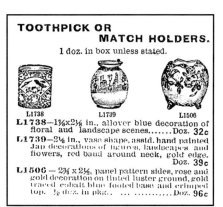

TOOTHPICK OR MATCH HOLDERS.
1 doz. in box unless stated.

L1738 L1739 L1506

L1738—1¾x2½ in., allover blue decoration of floral and landscape scenes......Doz. 32c

L1739—2½ in., vase shape, asstd. hand painted Jap decorations of figures, landscapes and flowers, red band around neck, gold edge. Doz. 39c

L1506 — 2¾ x 2½, panel pattern sides, rose and gold decoration on tinted luster ground, gold traced cobalt blue footed base and crimped top. ½ doz. in pkg. ....Doz. 96c

Nippon Sets

The following is a list of items that may be found in Nippon sets as listed in old catalog ads.

After-dinner coffee set – also called a demitasse set, consists of a tall pot with a long spout, cups, saucers, and sometimes a tray and a creamer and sugar bowl.

Asparagus set (decorated with an asparagus motif) – master dish and smaller serving dishes.

Berry set – several types are found, one is a large bowl with six smaller bowls; the other is a large perforated bowl and underplate with small individual bowls or nappies. The Manning Bowman set has a bowl and metal holder, tray, sugar and creamer.

Beverage set – a covered beverage container and matching tumblers.

Bread and butter set – large dish (approx. 7½" wide) and smaller butter pats about 3½" wide.

Bread and milk set – plate, bowl, and cream pitcher.

Breakfast set – adult size can be made up of an individual size coffee pot, individual chocolate pot, egg cup, pancake server, breakfast plate, cup and saucer, creamer and sugar bowl, salt and pepper; child's size, also called an oatmeal set or a bread and milk set, consists of a bowl, pitcher, and plate.

Bridge set – set of four ashtrays and sometimes a matching tray and cigarette holder.

Butter set – same as a bread and butter set, consists of a larger plate and butter pats; some old ads refer to this as a jelly set.

Cake set – larger serving dish and smaller matching plates.

Celery set – celery tray and individual salts.

Cheese and cracker set – round attached underplate containing a small bowl in the center with a cover. It can also be found with a perforated insert that is placed inside on top of ice chips to keep the cheese cold.

Chip and dip set – similar to cheese and cracker set but does not have a perforated insert.

Chocolate set – tall pot with a short spout at the top, cups, saucers, and sometimes a tray.

Cider set – a pitcher and matching tumblers, also called a lemonade set.

Coaster set – six to eight individual coasters.

Condiment set – mustard jar with spoon, salt and pepper shakers, toothpick holder, and tray.

Console set – also called a mantle set, consists of a bowl and often a pair of candlesticks and vases or an urn or two side urns.

Cordial set — also called a liquor or decanter set, made up of a decanter and pedestal glasses, often has a matching tray.

Corn set – a master dish (decorated with ears of corn) and smaller serving dishes just big enough for an ear of corn.

Creamer and sugar set – sugar bowl and creamer.

Cruet set – also called an oil and vinegar set, has oil and vinegar containers; sometimes has a salt and pepper and matching tray.

Decanter set – also called a liquor or cordial set, made up of a decanter and pedestal glasses, often has a matching tray.

Demitasse set – also called an after-dinner coffee set, consists of a pot, cups, saucers, and sometimes a matching tray and creamer and sugar bowl.

Desk set – tray letter holder, stamp box, ink blotter, calendar holder, inkwell with insert and blotter corners.

Dessert set – several individual plates that have an indentation for a cup, also called a snack, sandwich, refreshment, or toast set.

Dinner set – can consist of many pieces, dinner plates, breakfast plates, salad plates, cream soup bowls, bouillon cups and saucers, fruit saucers, cups and saucers, after-dinner cups and saucers, oatmeal dishes, small platter, medium platter, large platter, sugar bowl and cream pitcher, pickle dish, sauce or gravy boat, covered casserole or baker, covered serving dish, open vegetable dish, cake plate, salad plate, teapot, covered butter dish, coasters, celery dish and individual salts, and butter pats. There is also a child's play dinner set made up of a serving platter, covered casserole, dinner plates, cups and saucers, covered teapot, and sugar bowl and creamer.

Dresser set – can consist of a brush and comb, tray, hatpin holder, cologne bottle, pin tray, perfume bottle, trinket dish or box, stickpin holder, powder box, hair receiver, ring tree, hairpin holder, and sometimes a pair of candlesticks.

Fish set – large platter and small individual size plates; dishes are found in the shape of a fish or are decorated with fish scenes.

Fruit set – tray, pedestal bowl, and individual pedestal small bowls, similar to a punch set but smaller in size.

Game set – large serving platter and smaller serving plates, decorated with scenes of wild game.

Hostess set – also called a sweetmeat set, consists of a covered lacquer box with several individual dishes that fit inside.

Ice cream set – main serving dish and smaller bowls or plates, generally the tray is oblong and the plates are square.

Jelly set – larger plate and six individual dishes; old ads also call these butter or nut sets.

Lemonade set – pitcher and matching tumblers, also called a cider set.

Liquor set – also called a cordial or decanter set, made up of a decanter and pedestal glasses, often has a matching tray.

Lobster set – two-piece item made up of a bowl and underplate decorated with lobsters.

Luncheon set – similar to a dinner set, with a smaller luncheon plate but no dinner plates, does not contain all of the items in a complete dinner set. An old ad lists the following pieces: teapot, six bread and butter plates, six table plates, a sugar and creamer, berry bowl, six cups and saucers, six sauce dishes, six individual butter plates.

Manicure set – tray, powder box and different size jars that could be used for cold cream, powdered pumice, cuticle-ice, etc.

Mantle set – also called a console set, consists of a bowl, and often a pair of candlesticks and vases, urn, or two side urns.

Mayonnaise set – bowl, underplate and often a matching ladle, also called a whip cream set.

Milk set – milk pitcher and matching tumblers.

Nut set – medium size bowl and smaller ones to hold nuts; some are even found decorated with a nut motif.

Oatmeal set – also called a child's breakfast set or bread and milk set, consists of a bowl, small pitcher and plate.

Oil and vinegar set – also called a cruet set, has oil and vinegar containers and sometimes a salt and pepper and matching tray.

Open salt and pepper set – tray, pepper shaker and open salt dish.

Punch bowl set – punch bowl (often found with a pedestal base) contains a punch bowl and matching cups.

Refreshment set – also called a dessert, snack, sandwich, or toast set, consists of several individual plates that have an indentation for a cup; each plate comes with a matching cup.

Relish set – main serving dish is smaller than a celery dish; set includes individual salts.

Salad set – large bowl and smaller matching bowls, nappies, or plates; some sets even come with porcelain serving utensils, a long-handled fork and spoon.

Salt and pepper set – salt shaker or open salt and pepper shaker.

Sandwich set – also called a refreshment, snack, toast, or dessert set; it's a two-piece item consisting of a cup and matching plate that has an indentation for holding the cup.

Seasoning set – tray, oil and vinegar cruets, salt and pepper shakers, and a mustard jar and spoon.

Sherbet set – tray and a set of metal containers that hold small porcelain bowls for sherbet.

Smoke set (smoker's set) – tray, ashtray, humidor, tobacco jar, match holder, cigarette, cigar holder.

Stacked tea set – teapot, tea tile, creamer and sugar bowl that stack on one another.

Sweetmeat set – also called a hostess set, consists of a covered lacquer box with several individual dishes that fit inside.

Table set – sugar, creamer, butter dish, spoon holder.

Tankard set – tankard and matching mugs or steins.

Tea set – adult size contains teapot, cups, saucers, sugar bowl, creamer, and sometimes a matching tray. Children's play size and doll size can have same items. Old ads indicate that some children's sets came with only two, three or four cups and saucers, and some came with six.

Tête-à-tête set – teapot, sugar bowl, creamer, two cups and saucers.

Toast set – also referred to as a dessert, refreshment, sandwich or snack set. Set consists of several individual plates that have an indentation for a cup; each plate comes with a matching cup.

Vanity set – two perfume bottles and a powder box.

Whip cream set – also referred to as a mayonnaise set, with bowl, underplate, matching ladle.

Moriage Swans

By Jess Berry

The moriage technique was used to enhance many Nippon pieces, on some quite extensively while on others as highlight or accent. One of the most appealing uses is the Moriage Flying Swans design.

This design has been previously referred to as "Moriage Flying Geese" by most Nippon collectors; however, recent research reveals that it is based on a design used by another china manufacturer, the Worcester Porcelain Company of England, who copied it from a painting by Charles Baldwyn.

Pieces in this pattern usually have a solid matte finish background and feature swans in full flight. The swans are done in moriage with varying degrees of enamel detailing. The shapes were cut out and applied to the piece to represent flocks of flying swans. On some items, additional slip-trailed decor was added, however, usually only as small V's to indicate swans at a distance. Rims and edges are beaded and sometimes have a thin line of moriage for accent.

Details on the swans are done with raised white enamel. On some, the entire swan will be closely defined with enamel feathering, while on others you find more moriage with only basic details. Sometimes the moriage will be lightly shaded with blue or gray, while on other pieces the moriage remains the natural gray-white color without shading.

This pattern is most often found on vases, however there are also plaques, plates, pitchers, tankards, mugs, humidors, and ferners; of course, there may be other items of which I'm unaware since unknown Nippon pieces are continually being found.

The most common background color is a smoked gray which makes an effect rather like a cloudy sky. Usually only moriage flying swans are featured with no additional design other than beaded edging. The number of swans used depends on the size of the item, from one lone swan on a 3" footed vase to nine flying around a bulky 14" bottle vase.

Another background color found is varying shades of blue, ranging from very pale to a bright robin's egg shade, all in matte finish; however, occasional pieces with the blue background will have a satin finish. To date, no items have been found with a cobalt background.

A third background is a sunset colored cloudy sky with the suggestion of a lake in the foreground reflecting the sunset shades. Items with this coloring are much more difficult to find than those with the gray or blue backgrounds. These pieces usually have less enamel detailing and more moriage showing on the bodies of the swans.

All pieces with the gray and sunset color background carry the blue mark #52, while those items with blue grounds are found with mark #70, mark #90, and in the case of the robin's egg blue vase, blue mark #52. A few of the blue pieces are found with moriage reeds on the lower portion of the vase below the swans.

An additional background color found very rarely is a pale lavender. Pieces in this color have some gold highlighting not found on the other background tones.

Occasionally a piece will be completely unmarked as is the case with a basket vase with blue satin background and a crocus vase with gray ground. An interesting point relating to marks is two vases identical in every way except for background color, one gray and the other blue; the gray has blue maple leaf, the blue carries Oriental China Nippon.

The swans are placed so they fly from right to left as you face the piece; however, as usual, there is an exception. On a few of the blue vases, they go from left to right.

Are Moriage Flying Swan pieces a rarity? To that I'd answer both yes and no. They aren't extremely rare, but they are indeed difficult to locate, though marvelous examples do surface from time to time.

Enameling on Nippon

By Judith Boyd

Enameling was one type of paint used to good effect on Nippon. Heavy enameling on china provides texture and definition to the design. The build-up of glossy enamel on a Nippon piece gives a three-dimensional look that enhances its visual interest.

Enamel is a painting material composed of colored glass. There are four types of enamel that are made commercially — the opaque, the transparent or translucent, the opalescent, and the overglazes or over-painting enamels. Opaque enamels are solid colors which cover completely. The transparent and over-glaze types allow light, or other colors, to show through. "Flux" is a clear, colorless enamel that is the basis for all colored enamels. The primary ingredient is silica or sand. Potash or soda, plus lime, is added to make the clear form, then iron or lead oxide colors it.

Enameling on Nippon was used in different ways. Cloisonné was reproduced on porcelain to resemble the more-familiar metal cloisonné. A heavy build-up of enamel was used, much like moriage, to emphasize a design. Pottery-like designs were also produced with raised, enamel glazing. Enamel was also used on Nippon for all types of beading. This shiny decoration is found on a myriad of pieces.

The cloisonné pieces were produced by separating the colors in the design with copper or other soft-metal wires. Enamel was then carefully applied. When the piece was fired, the copper, enamel and porcelain all fused. Nippon pieces made with this technique are rare and difficult to find. If you are lucky enough to own a piece, please remember that this type of decoration is very fragile. It should be handled and cleaned with extreme care.

Imitation cloisonné can also be found on Nippon pieces. Thin lines of gold tracing simulated the wires to give the cloisonné effect. The enamel is built up in "cells" inside the gold. The familiar butterfly, on the blue marbleized background, is an example of this type of work (photo 1, p.59). On some pieces, imitation cloisonné was used for border decoration.

Heavy enameling has been used on Nippon to produce both geometric and scenic designs. It is glassy to the eye and slick to the touch. If you feel the design with your fingers, it is definitely raised (photo 2, p. 59). Do not confuse it with either moriage or blown-out decorating techniques. Moriage work consists of separate pieces of clay that have been applied to the main body. Blown-out work is actually pushed out from the inside, and is accomplished in the mold, not with paint.

Nippon with heavy enamel work often resembles pottery. The most common examples (and I use the word "common" advisedly) are in bright, primary colors (photo 3, p. 59). Art Nouveau and Art Deco designs that imitate the work of the Gouda Pottery Company of Holland were also made.

Enamel paint was also piled onto a piece to depict scenes. This is easy to confuse with moriage. Look carefully! Moriage is pebbly-looking and rough to the touch. Enamel is usually brightly colored.

The pieces decorated with the "Woodland" scene are one good example of the effects of enameling. Notice the bright and shiny reds and yellows on the leaves of the trees. Some scenic renditions with piled-up enamel resemble Satsuma.

Other pieces may have heavy enamel paint decoration surrounding the main picture, like a frame (photo 4, p. 59). Flowers, berries, or leaves in stand-out bright enamel sometimes overhang the bordered scene. Heavy gold decoration was also used in this manner.

Blobs of enamel were used as "jewels" in many designs (photo 5, p. 59). Large glass beads were used in a similar way to decorate stained-glass windows. These large "jewels" are often an integral part of the design.

Small dots of enamel were used as "beaded" decoration (also photo 5). Once again, do not confuse the "beads" with dots and strips of moriage. Gold was the predominant color, but many other colors were also used. Pieces that have been lavishly covered with enamel beads are prized by collectors. Turquoise beads on a gold background are particularly desirable.

Look through your collection and you will see how the use of enameling enhances the beauty of Nippon.

1. Cracker jar, 8½" wide, mark #47.

2. Vase, 12¼" tall, unmarked.

3. Vase, 9½" tall, mark #47.

4. Vase, 9½" tall, mark #47.

5. Example of both jeweling and beaded decoration.

Rectangular Wall Plaques

There are hundreds of round wall plaques to be found, but to date I have only been able to document 14 rectangular plaques. Twelve are handpainted and two are relief molded (blown-out); the two molded ones are plates #1468 and #2598 (see below). Most appear to be "framed" where the pattern extends to the edges. All are extremely desirable and becoming expensive to purchase, especially the relief molded ones. Only a handful are known to exist, and it is the lucky collector who owns one.

#2598

#1468

At the Old Ball Game

By Judith Boyd

During the Nippon era, the game of baseball flourished and became "America's National Pastime." Baseball legends such as Cy Young, Ty Cobb, John McGraw, Casey Stengel, and Walter Johnson slugged and pitched their way to immortality. Bankers and bricklayers, farmers and financiers populated the stands, rooting all together for their home town teams.

Semi-pro and amateur leagues were formed all over the country. Big businesses happily sponsored teams. Many in management believed it "provided a healthy way to fill spare time that might otherwise be devoted to Labor agitation – and taught immigrant workers how to be 'real' Americans." Women had their own leagues, the famous and hard-driving "Negro" Leagues were begun, and even prisoners played carefully supervised games.

The years 1891 to 1921 marked a period when many people left rural areas and flocked to the cities for financial reasons. The open fields of baseball diamonds provided a return to rural pleasures for people driven off the farm.

The first official baseball team, the New York Knickerbockers, was formed in 1845. In 1899, the American League was formed to challenge the existing National League. The first World Series was played in 1903 in Boston — with Cy Young pitching for Boston.

In 1950, Albert Spaulding convened a commission to prove baseball was an American invention. With dubious proof, they declared it had been "designed and named baseball" by Abner Doubleday one afternoon in 1839, in Cooperstown, N.Y. Spaulding declared that proved that baseball was truly America's National Game.

The designers of Nippon, obviously looking to cash in on an American love affair, used baseball as a theme for a few Nippon patterns.

Among the most interesting is a baseball glove with a bat laying across it (Figure 1). Given the relative disparity in real life proportions between a glove and a bat, the glove must have belonged to King Kong. The glove is marked "Baltimore Orioles." The Baltimore Orioles dominated the National League during the 1890s, winning three championships. The Boston Beaneaters were their hated rivals during that time. When the new American League was formed, Baltimore dropped out of the National League and joined the American League. The Boston Red Sox opened Fenway Park in 1912, the middle of the Nippon era. Like the Nippon that lines our shelves, Fenway Park still exists today – a little battered, somewhat worn, but still in use.

Note the uniforms on our Nippon baseball players (Figure 2). The baggy wools would never be worn by our sleek double-knit wearing heroes of today. Only the distinctive baseball cap has remained relatively unchanged for more than a century. Also note the faces of our Nippon players, particularly on the humidor. The fierce-eyed, cursing, tobacco-spitting ballplayer has been depicted as a slightly goofy-looking softie.

The children on the plates and cups (Figure 3) and particularly the little doll (Figure 4), depict the true spirit of baseball, then and now. No matter how many professional teams are playing, or how much money is involved, the real sport is still on the faces of the children playing on the sandlots, just as they have done for years.

The end of the Nippon era marked the "end of innocence" for baseball. In 1919, the infamous Chicago 'Black Sox' scandal scarred the reputation of professional baseball.

By 1921, however, Babe Ruth was slamming home runs for the New York Yankees and a new and more regulated time had begun for baseball.

Nippon china began a new era then as well. The familiar Nippon mark was replaced by a government-ordered "Made in Japan" and Nippon as we knew it was gone.

One Nippon tea set has an adorable scene of children playing football (Figure 5). At least, it appears similar to a football. Professional football was virtually non-existent during the Nippon era. College football, however, originally played in only a few Eastern schools, became popular during this time. From 1901 to 1904, Michigan's team led the nation. They were so powerful that they were known as the "point-a-minute" football team. Jim Thorpe played for the tiny Carlisle Indian School. His magnificent athleticism enabled them to demolish such great teams as Army and Penn.

Although football is a rough sport today, it was much more dangerous then. In 1905, 19 college and high school players were killed. President Theodore Roosevelt, an enthusiastic sportsman himself, invited a group of college presidents to the White House. They drew up a set of more humane rules to prevent further tragedy. Obviously, our sweet little Nippon children were not so violent.

One little Nippon girl appears to be carrying a badminton racquet under her arm (Figure 6). A shuttlecock is flying through the air, although she appears to be paying no attention to it. This was a relatively new sport, first played in 1873 in Badminton, Gloucestershire, England. The sport eventually traveled to the Western Hemisphere, where it caught on, but never achieved the popularity of tennis.

Two hunters and a pheasant can be seen on a rare Nippon plaque depicting this sport (Figure 7). Note the period clothes of our hunters, including their jaunty headgear. Hunting, of course, is an activity that began with mankind's first attempt to feed himself and has become a sport, instead of a necessity, only in modern times. The hunters pictured on our Native American Nippon pieces seem to be taking their hunting more seriously. The English Fox Hunt, also pictured on Nippon pieces, was imported to this country and continues to be popular, particularly in Virginia.

Horse racing is another ancient sport that continues to be enjoyed through our time (Figure 8). A Nippon humidor conveys the excitement of the stretch run, although the cheering throngs are left to our imagination.

Golf came to North America during the Nippon era. On Washington's birthday in 1888, the legendary first golf game was played. John Reid, dubbed the "Father of Golf in America," brought clubs from Scotland and founded the St. Andrews Golf Club in Yonkers, NY. In 1894, the first golf bags were used and golf courses were being constructed up and down the East Coast. The dress code was strict – spats, knickers, plaid shirts, and bow ties were commonly worn.

As the Nippon era progressed, the game of golf quickly became a symbol of the good life in America. By 1908, even President William H. Taft was playing.

The varied sports depicted on Nippon china reflect an historical view which helps us to picture contemporary life in the Nippon era.

BIBLIOGRAPHY

World Book Encyclopedia

Baseball – An Illustrated History. Geoffrey C. Ward and Ken Burns, Alfred A. Knopf, 1994.

This Fabulous Century, 1900 – 1910 and 1910 – 1920. Time Life Books

Golf in America – The First One Hundred Years. George Peper, Harry N. Abrams, Inc., NY, 1988.

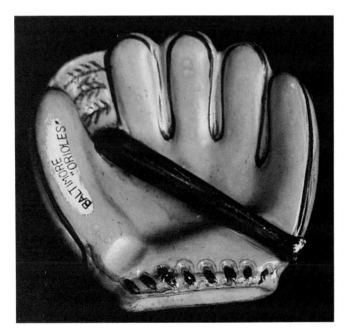

Figure 1. Novelty item.

Figure 2. Humidor.

Figure 2.

Front side of cup.

Figure 3. Feeding dish and bowl, rising sun mark.

Back side showing a doll.

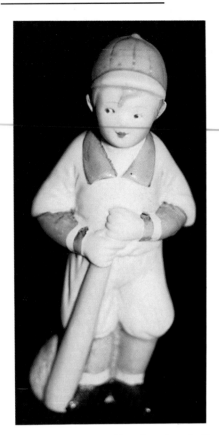

Figure 4. Above: Figurine, baseball player.

Novelty piece baseball player, rising sun mark.

Figure 5. Close-up of tea pot.

Below: Child's tea set.

Figure 6. Child's dishes and mug.

Figure 7. Hanging plaque.

Figure 9. Smoke set.

Figure 8. Humidor.

Reverse side of humidor.

Nippon Dog Items

By Jess Berry

Dogs were a popular subject used on Nippon items, especially on plaques, humidors, ashtrays, and jugs. As with most portrait type decor, some were fully hand-painted while others made use of decals for the dog with hand-painted background treatment and trim. Of particular interest are two series or sets in the Nippon dog pieces group.

One series consists of six different dogs used on three different size plaques, 8", 9", and 10" diameters. The 8" and 10" plaques are identical except for size, and have a green border trimmed with heavy enameling in a daisy-like design. The 9" uses a different border with the dog framed in a medallion-type center. The dogs are done with decals, borders are hand-painted, and all three sized plaques have lots of jewels and beading.

Decals used on both the 8" and 9" plaques are the same size, while the one used on the 10" plaque is considerably larger. All dogs are shown head and neck view only. These plaques are marked with the blue maple leaf mark.

The other series features champion bulldogs; there are four different views used. Items found in this group are 10" plaques, whiskey jugs, humidors, cigarette boxes, and two styles of ashtrays. The decals show the entire dog, and in some cases, list his name at the bottom, though this is inconsistent from piece to piece. The bulldogs are identified as Champion L'Ambassadeur, Champion Rodney Stone, Champion Katerfelto, and Champion Bromley Crib, champion bulldogs from the 1895 – 1905 era. Of the four, Champion L'Ambassadeur is the one most commonly found and Champion Katerfelto seems to be the most difficult to locate.

The plaques, humidors, boxes, and one style ashtray are decorated with a dark brown geometric trim on cream background, while the whiskey jugs have a brown marbled all-over background with the dog displayed in a beaded frame. The round ashtray has a less bold brown design on a cream background. All items in this series are marked with the green M-in-wreath mark.

In addition to these two series, there are some magnificent 12" fully hand-painted plaques, as well as other various pieces featuring a variety of dogs. They all make attractive additions to a Nippon collection.

These photos show the six different dogs found on the three sizes of wall plaques. These are all 9" wall plaques and each bears the blue maple leaf #52 backstamp.

Same dog, all three sizes of wall plaques, 10", 9", and 8". All have blue maple leaf backstamp #52.

Three of the other dogs on two sizes of wall plaques. All bear the blue maple leaf backstamp #52.

10" plaques. Each dog is a decal. All have the green M-in-wreath, mark #47. Champion Rodney Stone; Champion L'Ambassadeur and Champion Bromley Crib.

Cigarette boxes. Both have the green M-in-wreath backstamp #47. Champion Katerfelto and Champion Rodney Stone.

12" wall plaque. Fully hand-painted, bears the green M-in-wreath, backstamp #47.

10" wall plaque. Decal of Newfoundland dog, bears the green M-in-wreath, backstamp #47. Adapted from painting by Sir Edwin Landseer.

Whiskey Jugs. All three are backstamped with the green M-in-wreath, mark #47. Champion Bromley Crib, Champion L'Ambassadeur; and Champion Rodney Stone.

This photo shows the variety of items that can be found bearing decals of the Champion dogs. All are marked with the green M-in-wreath, backstamp #47. Hand-painted decor surrounds each dog decal.

Ashtray, 5½" wide, blue mark #52.

Rectangular wall plaque. Adapted from painting by Sir Edwin Landseer.

Molded in relief wall plaque, 10¾" wide, green mark #47.

Salesman sample page of plaque at left.

Nippon Dolls

The dictionary describes a doll as a child's toy image of a human being. Today's old Nippon dolls are adult toys and expensive ones at that. What once might have cost a few pennies will now fetch $100, $200, and more.

Most Nippon dolls were manufactured and imported during World War I when dolls were not imported from Germany. Among the companies importing these dolls were Langfelder; Homma and Hayward Inc.; Nippon Novelty Co.; Louis Wolf & Co.; Morimura Bros.; George Borgfeldt & Co.; and Butler Brothers.

In the all-bisque dolls we find copies of fairy tale characters, Little Red Riding Hood, for instance, baseball players, cave people, Oriental children, ballerinas, soldiers, brides and grooms, policemen, Dutch children, Indian maidens, and even leprechauns. The list goes on and on — such diversity!

Today, some of the larger bisque head dolls will be found with original mohair wigs, glass eyes, composition bodies, sleep eyes, open-close mouths with painted tongues and teeth. Those with character faces are the most highly sought of the Nippon bisque head dolls.

The Nippon backstamp can often be found on the back of the doll between the shoulders or sometimes on the feet. On bisque head dolls, the mark is found on the back of the head and neck.

Bisque doll heads were made in molds which were used approximately 30 to 50 times and then discarded. The eye sockets were cut out with a special tool. Some of the larger heads had applied ears; many of the smaller ones had the ears cast right in the mold. During the firing, the doll heads or limbs lost about one-seventh of their volume from shrinkage. Doll makers could use this shrinkage to make another mold of the fired, smaller head and/or limbs which produced a head one-seventh smaller each time the process was repeated.

The only patents I've been able to find for Nippon dolls are the ones for the Dolly Doll and Queue San Baby, both manufactured by Morimura Bros. In 1917 Frederick Langfelder designed the Dolly doll and assigned the rights to Morimura Bros. As you will note, the actual doll in the photo varies somewhat from the drawing shown in the patent. The Dolly label is much larger than drawn and the face is different in appearance. The legs are together in the sketch and the Dolly sticker is smaller and placed nearer to the waistline.

Queue San Baby was designed by Hikozo Araki and patented on Feb. 29, 1916, #48,625. Araki was an assignor to Morimura Bros.

Collectors can also find a kneeling Queue San Baby and a fully jointed Queue San Baby but neither doll's patent has been located. Queue San Baby means baby or doll with a queue (braid).

A number of half dolls were made into pincushions and originally sold for 75¢ to $4.00 a dozen.

German dolls reappeared on the U.S. scene by 1922 and Morimura Bros. stopped handling dolls soon after.

Collectors should always save the old clothes they find the dolls dressed in, even if the clothing is changed by the new owner. Another collector may someday want the older clothes. Original boxes add to the value, so they should not be discarded. Many of the small bisque dolls need careful cleaning. The skin coloring was often not fired on and will wash off very easily. You might end up with a pale doll.

Known Nippon Era Dolls

Baby Bud (see Plate 134), originally made in Germany but all bisque versions were also made in Japan.

Baby Darling (see Plate 137), imported by Morimura Bros. beginning in 1919, it's an all-bisque doll with a sticker on its stomach.

Baby Doll (see Plate 2328) sold by Montgomery Ward, toddler composition body, painted shoes and socks.

Baby Ella, imported by Morimura from 1918 – 1921, fully jointed body with a bisque head, varies in size from 6½" to 23".

Baby Lucy has a bisque head with sleeping eyes, 10" to 18" in size, imported in 1918 – 1921 by Tajimi Co. and Taiyo Trading Co.

Baby O' Mine, imported by Morimura Bros. in 1920.

Baby Rose, imported by Morimura Bros. from 1919 – 1921, all-bisque doll, sticker on stomach.

Chubby, all-bisque small doll, imported between 1914 – 1916 by Louis Wolf & Co.

Dolly (see Plate 631), this doll was patented by Langfelder for Morimura in 1917, Dolly sticker on front.

First Prize Baby was distributed by Morimura Bros. during 1919 – 1920.

Happifats (see Plate 2359), comes in both male and female versions; it is a copy of the 1914 German doll, rotund bodies and molded clothes.

Jollikid (see plates 135 and 686), comes in both male and female versions, all-bisque doll with molded clothes.

Kewpie (see Plate 677), designed by Rose O'Neill in 1912, the Nippon doll was the Japanese version of the original.

Ladykin (see Plate 685), small all-bisque doll with molded dress and ribbon in her hair

Manikin (see Plate 2371), small, all-bisque doll with molded clothing.

My Darling is another name for Baby Darling.

Queue San Baby (see Plate 637), designed by Hikozo Araki in 1915, registered in 1916, sold between 1915 – 1922 by Morimura Bros.

Sonny (see Plate 673), all-bisque, molded socks and shoes.

Doll Glossary

All-bisque doll – (pretty self-explanatory), generally small in size (under 7"), most are jointed at shoulders and/or hips.

Baby dolls – represent small children or babies, dolls preferred by young children.

Ball-jointed body – usually a composition doll body that permits the doll joint to move in all directions, composed of a ball and two adjacent sockets strung with a metal spring or elastic at the knees or hips and shoulders.

Bathtub Baby – small all-bisque doll in sitting position found in small bisque tub.

Bisque head – self-explanatory, some have an open mouth, others have a closed mouth, some have teeth, rest of the body is of another type of material, such as cloth, kid, or composition.

Bonnet dolls – bisque head with molded bonnet/hat.

Breast plate doll's head – usually called shoulder plate dolls, doll's head with shoulders attached to the head; usually found with cloth or kid bodies.

Breathers – doll heads with pierced nostrils.

Candy Store doll – originally sold on cards, 12 dolls to a card in many instances, these are small, all bisque dolls.

Character doll – lifelike representation of a child, baby or real person.

China head – glossy in appearance, not bisque looking, most Nippon ones will be found having blonde hair; usually has a cloth body.

Closed mouth doll – doll heads whose lips are together, not parted with teeth, sometimes called a "pouty."

Composition body — the body is composed of a mixture prepared by the maker, each had their own formula but some were made of wood, glue, and pulp mixture.

Flirting Eyes – eyes that move from side to side instead of opening and shutting.

Half doll – just the upper half of a doll, from the waist up, more elegant type ladies, often used for the top of a pin cushion, tea cozy, etc., highly glazed.

Intaglio eyes – painted eyes with concave iris and pupil.

Kid body – made from tanned sheepskin.

Kidaline or Kidolyn body – line of dolls imported by Morimura Bros., these are imitation kid bodies.

Marks and numbers – it's believed that some are for production reference, some may tell the size, they usually identify the maker and mold type.

Nostrils – some heads can be found with pierced noses and are called breathers, but most Nippon dolls will just be found with two dots marking the area.

Open/close mouth – parted lips that have no opening, there is an area showing between them that is either white or pink. The mouth may look open but there is no actual hole. Some will be found with molded teeth or a tongue.

Shoulder plate dolls – See breast plate dolls.

Sleeping eyes – eyes that open and close, usually made of glass.

Dolly Doll (see Plate 631).

DESIGN.
F. LANGFELDER.
DOLL.
APPLICATION FILED JULY 26, 1917.

51,387.   Patented Oct. 16, 1917.

Fig. 3

Fig. 2

Fig. 1

Inventor
Frederick Langfelder
by his atty Charles G. Handy

UNITED STATES PATENT OFFICE.

FREDERICK LANGFELDER, OF NEW YORK, N. Y., ASSIGNOR TO MORIMURA BROS., OF NEW YORK, N. Y., A FIRM COMPOSED OF ICHIZAEMON MORIMURA, ESTATE OF TOYO MORIMURA, SANEYOSKI HIROSE, SENEMITSU HIROSE, AND YUSAKATA MURAI.

DESIGN FOR A DOLL.

51,387.   Specification for Design.   Patented Oct. 16, 1917.

Application filed July 26, 1917.   Serial No. 182,987.   Term of patent 7 years.

To all whom it may concern:

Be it known that I, FREDERICK LANG-FELDER, a citizen of the United States, residing in the city, county, and State of New York, have invented a new, original, and ornamental Design for Dolls, of which the following is a specification, reference being had to the accompanying drawing, forming part thereof.

Figure 1 is a front elevation of a doll, showing my new design, Fig. 2 is a side elevation thereof and Fig. 3 is a rear elevation thereof.

I claim:

The ornamental design for a doll, as shown.

FREDERICK LANGFELDER.

Copies of this patent may be obtained for five cents each, by addressing the "Commissioner of Patents, Washington, D. C."

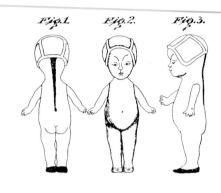

DESIGN.

H. ARAKI.
DOLL.
APPLICATION FILED NOV. 10, 1915.

48,625.

Patented Feb. 29, 1916.

Fig.1   *Fig.2*   *Fig.3*

Witnesses: Inventor
C. S. Ashley   Hikozo Araki
Henry M. Urse   By his Attorneys
                              Urse + Buttenstein

Queue San Baby (Plate 673).

UNITED STATES PATENT OFFICE.

HIKOZO ARAKI, OF BROOKLYN, NEW YORK, ASSIGNOR TO MORIMURA BROS., OF NEW YORK, N. Y., A FIRM COMPOSED OF ITCHIZAEMON MORIMURA, YASUKATA MURAI, AND SANEHIDE HIROSE.

DESIGN FOR A DOLL.

48,625.   Specification for Design.   Patented Feb. 29, 1916.

Application filed November 10, 1915.   Serial No. 60,794.   Term of patent 3½ years.

To all whom it may concern:

Be it known that I, HIKOZO ARAKI, a subject of the Emperor of Japan, and residing at 417 Monroe street, in the borough of Brooklyn, county of Kings, and State of New York, have invented a new, original, and ornamental Design for a Doll, of which the following is a specification, reference being had to the accompanying drawing, forming part thereof.

Figure 1 is a back view; Fig. 2 a front view and Fig. 3 a side view of the doll showing my new design:

I claim:

The ornamental design for a doll as shown.

HIKOZO ARAKI.

Witnesses:
J. C. LAWRENCE,
C. W. COWLES.

Copies of this patent may be obtained for five cents each, by addressing the "Commissioner of Patents, Washington, D. C."

"BABY BUD" BISQUE DOLLS

A chubby little figure with roguish expression and arms that can be moved with many cute poses.

Fine flesh tinted bisque, painted features, roguish eyes, exposed tongue, short shirt, movable position arms which give different expressions at each pose, each in box.

F9806—4 in. 1 doz. in pkg.
Doz. **$1.35**

F9808—6¾ in. ½ doz. in pkg.
Doz. **$3.75**

"WIDE-AWAKE" DOLLS.

"Wide-awake" —Fine bisque, tinted hair and features, large eyes, open mouth showing 2 teeth, chubby bodies, jointed arms, painted footwear. Boxes with illustrated covers and nursery rhymes.

F7786—4¾ in. ½ doz. in box, 1 doz. in pkg
Doz. Out

F7787—6¼ in. Each in box, ½ doz. in pkg.
Doz. **$2.75**

Butler Bros. catalog ads

PENNY SOLID CHINA DOLL

White china body painted features, blonde and brunette hair. 1 gro. in box.

F9780—1¾ in.
Gro. **65c**

F9781—2½ in.
Gro. **89c**

GLAZED SOLID CHINA DOLL

F8175 — 2 in., glazed white body, painted features, hair, shoes and stockings. 6 doz. in box.............Doz. **22c**
(Total **$1.32**)

1920 Butler Bros. ad.

CHINA DOLL PIN CUSHION

Regular 25c Size

N1522—1½x⅞ waistline china doll, 3¾x2½ over all, tinted hair, features and waist, worsted sash, bright red and green sateen skirt effect. Asstd. 3 doz. in box................Doz **75c**

Early Butler Bros. ad.

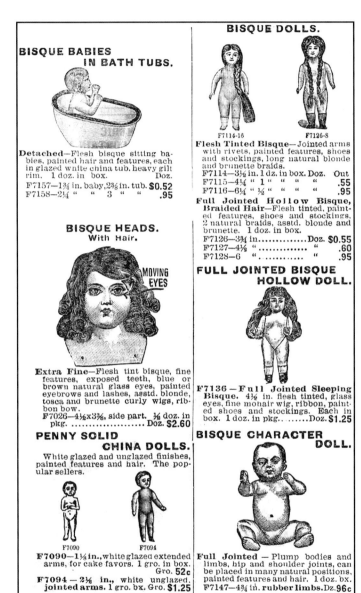

BISQUE BABIES IN BATH TUBS.

Detached—Flesh bisque sitting babies, painted hair and features, each in glazed white china tub, heavy gilt rim. 1 doz. in box. Doz.
F7157—1¾ in. baby, 2⅜ in. tub. **$0.52**
F7158—2¼ "   "   3   "   "   **.95**

BISQUE HEADS.
With Hair.

MOVING EYES

Extra Fine—Flesh tint bisque, fine features, exposed teeth, blue or brown natural glass eyes, painted eyebrows and lashes, asstd. blonde, tosca and brunette curly wigs, ribbon bow.
F7026—4½x3⅜, side part. ⅙ doz. in pkg. .... Doz. **$2.60**

PENNY SOLID CHINA DOLLS.

White glazed and unglazed finishes, painted features and hair. The popular sellers.

F7090   F7094

F7090—1¼ in., white glazed extended arms, for cake favors. 1 gro. in box. Gro. **52c**

F7094—2½ in., white unglazed, jointed arms. 1 gro. bx. Gro. **$1.25**

BISQUE DOLLS.

F7114-16   F7126-8

Flesh Tinted Bisque—Jointed arms with rivets, painted features, shoes and stockings, long natural blonde and brunette braids.
F7114—3½ in. 1 dz. in box. Doz.   Out
F7115—4¼ " 1 " " " " .55
F7116—6¼ " ½ " " " " .95
Full Jointed Hollow Bisque, Braided Hair—Flesh tinted, painted features, shoes and stockings, 2 natural braids, asstd. blonde and brunette. 1 doz. in box.
F7126—3¾ in. .... Doz. **$0.55**
F7127—4½ " .... " .60
F7128—6 " .... " .95

FULL JOINTED BISQUE HOLLOW DOLL.

F7136 — Full Jointed Sleeping Bisque. 4½ in. flesh tinted, glass eyes, fine mohair wig, ribbon, painted shoes and stockings. Each in box. 1 doz. in pkg. .... Doz. **$1.25**

BISQUE CHARACTER DOLL.

Full Jointed — Plump bodies and limbs, hip and shoulder joints, can be placed in many natural positions, painted features and hair. 1 doz. bx.
F7147—4¾ in. rubber limbs. Dz. **96c**

Early Butler Bros. ad.

Butler Bros. catalog ads.

This small floral decorated covered jar was found in its original cardboard box and bearing beauty cream from the early 1900s era. The piece is 2" wide and bears the pagoda backstamp. Original papers inside read:

The Dame Standish Satin Cream.

A most satisfactory cold cream both for maintaining and cleaning the skin. May be left on the skin and practically disappears leaving no unpleasant sticky sensation – just a smooth satin like softness which gives one the satisfaction of being well groomed. This cream has the delightful look of the bayberries suggesting downs and fields and the cool sea breeze because it is made with the pure bayberrie wax which has long been known to have healing properties. It is the only cream made in this way with the bayberrie wax.

The Dame Standish Satin Cream will prevent sunburn and protect exposure if rubbed in lightly and dusted over with a pure simple powder. Gentlemen who use this cream after shaving prefer it to a cream which has a lingering hot house perfume.

The Dame Standish Satin Cream is superior in purity.

The Dame Standish Satin Cream is soothing and healing.

The Dame Standish Satin Cream keeps perfectly.

The Dame Standish Satin Cream makes the pores fine and the skin smooth.

The Dame Standish Satin Cream lasts well, for so little is necessary so it is economical and best of all, continual use of The Dame Standish Satin Cream makes the skin more beautiful and keeps it in perfect condition.

Evidently this cream was intended for both ladies and gentlemen. To locate an item like this intact with the cream is a real find and helps us discover more about the original uses of our Nippon items.

Royal Kinjo

Every now and then collectors will spot an item backstamped with the Royal Kinjo mark, patent No. 17705. Efforts to track down this patent have been futile until Aki Oga from Japan was able to acquire information. The patent is from the same time period as the coralene one but the technique is definitely different. Some collectors refer to it as salt glaze, orange peel, sharkskin, or sand finish. Although these items are not backstamped with the word Nippon, they are definitely from the so-called Nippon era.

There are very few Royal Kinjo items to be found. As lovely as they are, they were evidently not popular with the Western market or not profitable to produce. Rare is the collection that contains one of these items.

This Japanese patent was filed by Yasunosuke Doi, who is also the inventor. It was filed on October 18, 1909, and was allowed on February 26, 1910. The inventor's address was in Nagoya. Information about how long this patent was in effect is not available because records were destroyed in World War II.

The technique was the process of firing a dew-like surface on the porcelain. The specifications are as follows:

1. Draw an outline of a picture on a white porcelain body.
2. Fire the porcelain.
3. Put color on the picture.
4. Spray the steamed water on the surface of the porcelain, so at this stage there will be tiny water drops or dew on the surface.
5. Sprinkle in the glass powder on top of the porcelain.
6. Fire in the usual manner. The aim for this process is to easily and speedily make the dew-like surface more beautiful.

Four vases backstamped Royal Kinjo.

The Mystery Patent

Research has brought to light Japanese patent 16430 which was created by Toshio Soga of Nagoya City. The first page of the patent shows the front view and also the view from the top, looking down on the object. This object is ceramic ware with pearl shell. The paperwork for the patent was entered at the patent office on December 28, 1909 (the year Meiji 42 in Japan). The patent registration was given on March 5, 1910 (the year Meiji 43 in Japan). The translation reads that this is an example of tojiki or ceramic ware. Powdered pearl shell was used for the picture in the ceramic part. The second page is a cut view showing thickness, etc. The Japanese writing describes what is seen in the illustration. Using the Western-style alphabet, a Japanese translator has deciphered the following: (Readers should match the alphabet with the Japanese characters to get the meaning.)

This technique used powdered pearl shell on ceramic pieces. Whether these items made their way to American shores is not known at this time, but since this patent was registered in 1910, we can assume this was a time when new techniques were being tried. Our coralene and Royal Kinjo marked pieces are all from this time period. There are few coralene items to be found and even fewer Royal Kinjo wares. New and wonderful items are being found every day.

A (= イ) This is the basic part of the ceramic ware. It is the inside material.

B (= ロ) This is a paint that is raised, plus it has a design on it.

C (= ハ) A sticky glue-type of chemical plus a gluey agent.

D (= ニ) Powdered pearl shell

Key to page 2.

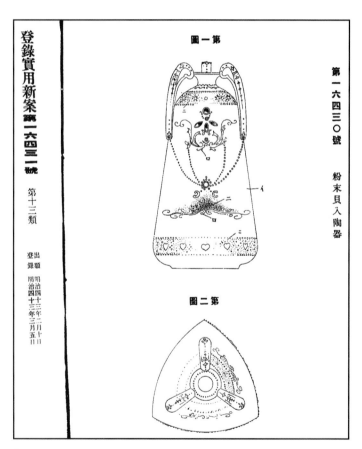

Page 1.

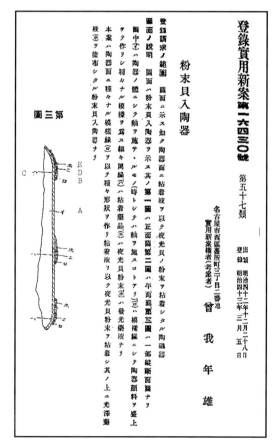

Page 2.

Translation of Page 2:
With all the above in place, next apply a liquid lacquer. Next comes a medical (? that's the best we could get from the Japanese character) fluid. Next comes a liquid that produces a luminous body. A liquid polisher that produces a glazed finish (luster or glossy finish). This system was also used to make many other styles and designs for pots, ceramic ware, etc.

Nippon Dinnerware Patents

Although most Nippon collectors do not collect dinnerware pieces, the following patents are included because they are part of our history and because so few Nippon era patents have been located.

All 20 of these were patented on August 2, 1921, by Teiji Kotato, assignor to the Morimura Bros. The application for each was filed on October 16, 1920, and the actual patterns were most likely used even before these dates.

Most of these patterns have been identified and a name ascribed. Some have Nippon backstamps, others Japan. Each patent shown is for a dinner plate from a china dinner set.

58581 The Ceylon*
58582 The Yale*
58583 Unknown
58584 Seville *
58585 Angora
58586 Beverly *
58587 Bellfonte*
58588 Alsace*
59589 Beverly
58590 The Sahara*
58591 Florencia
58592 Unknown
58593 Montclare
58594 Hanover
58595 Thelma
58596 Majestic
58597 The Argonne*
58598 Lafayette
58599 The Coniston
58600 Rembrandt

DESIGN.
T. KOTATO.
PLATE OR SIMILAR ARTICLE.
APPLICATION FILED OCT. 16, 1920.

58,581.   Patented Aug. 2, 1921.

*indicates that some pieces in these sets have been located with a Nippon era backstamp

UNITED STATES PATENT OFFICE.

TEIJI KOTATO, OF NEW YORK, N. Y., ASSIGNOR TO MORIMURA BROS., OF NEW YORK, N. Y., A FIRM COMPOSED OF SHIKAE MORIMURA, KAISAKU MORIMURA, SHIGEKI MORIMURA, ISAMU MORIMURA, SANEYOSHI HIROSE, MINORU TANAKA, YASU-KATA MURAI, TARU MURAI, AND EUNOSKE JINUSHI.

DESIGN FOR A PLATE OR SIMILAR ARTICLE.

58,581.   Specification for Design.   Patented Aug. 2, 1921.

Application filed October 16, 1920. Serial No. 417,501. Term of patent 7 years.

To all whom it may concern:

Be it known that I, TEIJI KOTATO, a subject of the Emperor of Japan, residing in the city, county, and State of New York, have invented a new, original, and ornamental Design for a Plate or Similar Article, of which the following is a specification, reference being had to the accompanying drawing, forming part hereof.

The figure is a plan view of one of the pieces, to wit: the dinner plate, of a china dinner set, showing my new design.

I claim:

The ornamental design for a plate or similar article, as shown.

TEIJI KOTATO.

DESIGN.

T. KOTATO.

PLATE OR SIMILAR ARTICLE.

APPLICATION FILED OCT. 16, 1920.

58,582.

Patented Aug. 2, 1921.

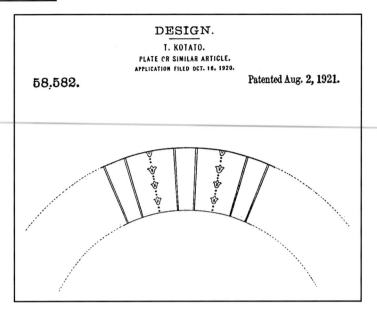

DESIGN.

T. KOTATO.

PLATE OR SIMILAR ARTICLE.

APPLICATION FILED OCT. 16, 1920.

58,583.

Patented Aug. 2, 1921.

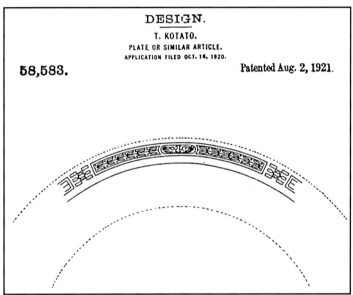

DESIGN.

T. KOTATO.

PLATE OR SIMILAR ARTICLE.

APPLICATION FILED OCT. 16, 1920.

58.584.

Patented Aug. 2, 1921.

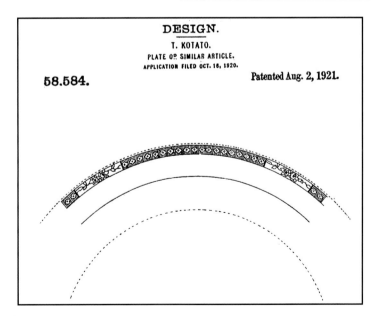

DESIGN.

T. KOTATO.

PLATE OR SIMILAR ARTICLE.

APPLICATION FILED OCT. 16, 1920.

8,585.

Patented Aug. 2, 1921.

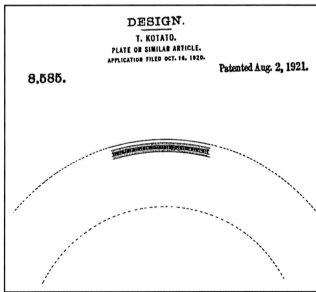

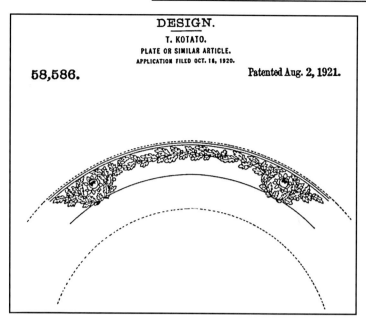

DESIGN.

T. KOTATO.

PLATE OR SIMILAR ARTICLE.

APPLICATION FILED OCT. 18, 1920.

58,586.

Patented Aug. 2, 1921.

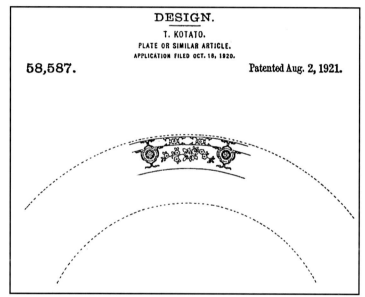

DESIGN.

T. KOTATO.

PLATE OR SIMILAR ARTICLE.

APPLICATION FILED OCT. 18, 1920.

58,587.

Patented Aug. 2, 1921.

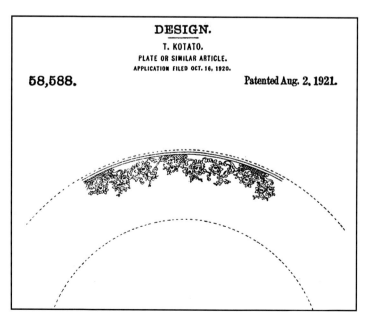

DESIGN.

T. KOTATO.

PLATE OR SIMILAR ARTICLE.

APPLICATION FILED OCT. 16, 1920.

58,588.

Patented Aug. 2, 1921.

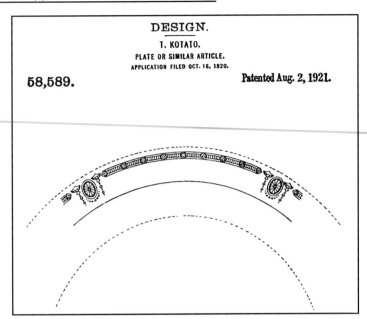

DESIGN.
T. KOTATO.
PLATE OR SIMILAR ARTICLE.
APPLICATION FILED OCT. 16, 1920.
58,589.
Patented Aug. 2, 1921.

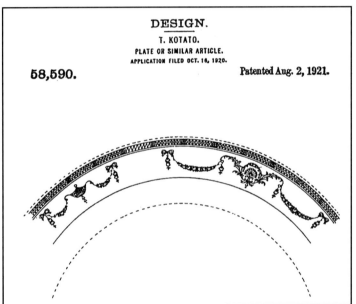

DESIGN.
T. KOTATO.
PLATE OR SIMILAR ARTICLE.
APPLICATION FILED OCT. 16, 1920.
58,590.
Patented Aug. 2, 1921.

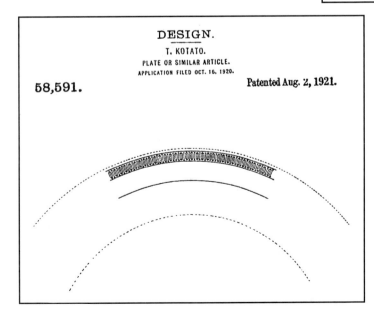

DESIGN.
T. KOTATO.
PLATE OR SIMILAR ARTICLE.
APPLICATION FILED OCT. 16, 1920.
58,591.
Patented Aug. 2, 1921.

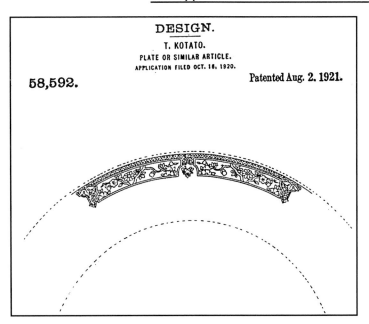

DESIGN.

T. KOTATO.

PLATE OR SIMILAR ARTICLE.

APPLICATION FILED OCT. 16, 1920.

58,592.

Patented Aug. 2. 1921.

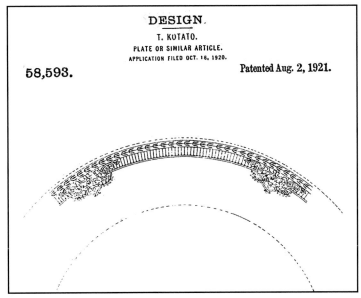

DESIGN.

T. KOTATO.

PLATE OR SIMILAR ARTICLE.

APPLICATION FILED OCT. 16, 1920.

58,593.

Patented Aug. 2, 1921.

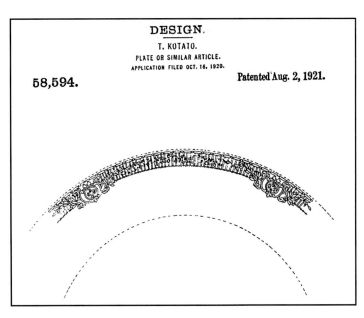

DESIGN.

T. KOTATO.

PLATE OR SIMILAR ARTICLE.

APPLICATION FILED OCT. 16, 1920.

58,594.

Patented Aug. 2, 1921.

DESIGN,
T. KOTATO.
PLATE OR SIMILAR ARTICLE.
APPLICATION FILED OCT. 16, 1920.

58,595.

Patented Aug. 2, 1921.

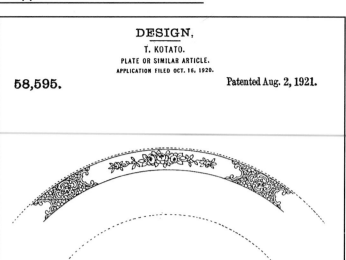

DESIGN.
T. KUTATO.
PLATE OR SIMILAR ARTICLE.
APPLICATION FILED OCT. 16, 1920.

58,596.

Patented Aug. 2, 1921.

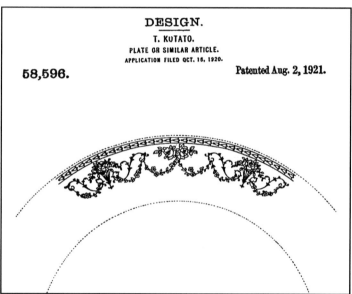

DESIGN.
T. KOTATO.
PLATE OR SIMILAR ARTICLE.
APPLICATION FILED JAN. 31, 1921.

58,597.

Patented Aug. 2, 1921.

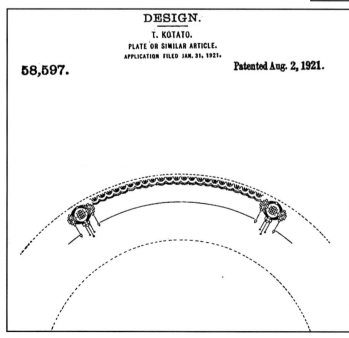

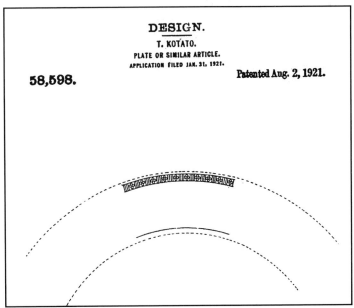

DESIGN.

T. KOTATO.

PLATE OR SIMILAR ARTICLE.

APPLICATION FILED JAN. 31, 1921.

58,598.

Patented Aug. 2, 1921.

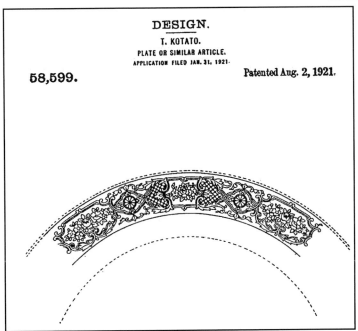

DESIGN.

T. KOTATO.

PLATE OR SIMILAR ARTICLE.

APPLICATION FILED JAN. 31, 1921.

58,599.

Patented Aug. 2, 1921.

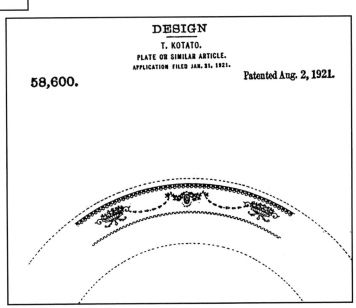

DESIGN

T. KOTATO.

PLATE OR SIMILAR ARTICLE.

APPLICATION FILED JAN. 31, 1921.

58,600.

Patented Aug. 2, 1921.

Nippon Inventory Sheet

It's always a good idea to have a complete inventory of your Nippon collection, including both photos and accompanying information. Since our porcelain pieces vary from other collectibles, I have devised an inventory sheet that should allow you to note all significant information.

Photocopy* this sheet and insert copies in a three-ring binder. Your current collection can be kept in the front part and items that have been sold in the back. Whenever items match pieces shown in *The Collector's Encyclopedia of Nippon Porcelain*, be sure to make a notation. Reappraise your items every few years and update these prices on your inventory sheet.

*Permission is given by the author to photocopy the inventory sheet for the personal use of collectors.

Nippon Inventory Sheet

**Place
Photo
Here**

Item(s) _____

Date Acquired _____

Purchased From _____

Price Paid $ _____

Description (height, width, diameter, etc.) _____

_____

_____

Pattern and/or technique used _____

_____

Collector's Encyclopedia of Nippon Porcelain reference #s:

If exact item, plate # _____

If not exact as shown:

Similar shape, plate # _____

Similar pattern or design, plate # _____

Additional information _____

_____

Condition_____

Backstamp # _____

Color of backstamp_____

Other:

Current Appraisals:

Date _____ Value $ _____

Date _____ Value $ _____

Date _____ Value $ _____

Date _____ Value $ _____

Date _____ Value $ _____

Date Sold_____

Selling Price _____

Sold To _____

Reproduction Alert

When the Fourth Series was published, more than 30 different fake patterns were included. Since then many more have surfaced. Most are obvious to the trained eye, but one new pattern has been manufactured which is fooling collectors everywhere. I purchased several reproduction pieces for this book and when I got them home from the wholesaler, I realized they were a knockoff of a genuine pattern. I had a creamer, sugar bowl, and candy bowl in this same pattern. The manufacturer in China had to have seen similar wares in person to do such a good job.

The genuine pieces bear the RC backstamp and are very delicate and beautiful. The new pieces are not as good, but I only paid $20 for the pair of candlesticks and less than $5 for the hatpin holder. From a distance it's difficult to tell them from the real thing. And if this wasn't bad enough, the M-in-wreath mark has now been faithfully copied.

The new figural piece discovered is referred to as a "Nippon black mammy toothpick holder" and has been advertised for sale for as much as $125.00. It has a Nippon mark on the bottom but it is definitely not a Nippon era (1891 – 1921) piece — it's brand new. It is not even a true reproduction – it's an outright fake. I know of no such Nippon piece in existence. This item is being pitched to both Nippon and black memorabilia collectors. A visit to the wholesaler will enable you to purchase it for $1.50. Buy six and you get a 10 percent discount. That's quite a profit.

The reproduction wholesalers are generally open only to dealers. If you ever get a chance to visit one, you will be shocked to find out what is available. Presently, I am afraid to buy most anything out of my area of expertise. Old sleighs, posters, signed Tiffany lamps, Christmas ornaments, depression glass, Roseville, Limoges, R.S. Prussia, the list goes on and on — all are available.

Close-up of genuine candy bowl.

Close-up of fake hatpin holder.

Top of sugar bowl. Notice the similarities to candy bowl.

Some of the reproduction wholesalers put disclaimers in their catalogs, stating that their items are merely reproductions and new in order to cover themselves. But if there is no intention to ultimately deceive someone, why would anyone bother to put a fake Nippon back stamp on the piece?

In some of their catalogs, you cannot tell how the fake item is backstamped, but others make it easy for the consumer. One outfit has a heading which says "Nippon collectibles — new arrivals" and each fake piece has an order number prefaced with the letters NIP.

Presently, the pieces I am aware of are being imported to wholesalers in the United States from both Japan and China. Wholesale prices run anywhere from $4 – $6.50 for hatpin holders; candlesticks cost around $10 – $15 each; vases are from $13 – $40 depending on size and decoration; tea sets can be as high as $95 with six cups and saucers; shaving mugs are about $10.00 and tankards are in the range of $70. All types of items are being sold, chocolate sets, butter dishes, urns, vases, bells, trinket boxes, cookie jars and perfume bottles to list a few. Our present customs rules allow these items into the country and I see no end in sight unless those rules are changed. If an item is marked in any way under the glaze, it should also identify the name of the importing country under the glaze. The McKinley Tariff Act was passed in 1890 and states that as of March 1, 1891, all articles of foreign manufacture shall be marked in legible English words so as to indicate the country of their origin. This was to be done as indelibly and permanently as the nature of the article would permit.

On February 8, 1917, the Treasury Department decided that chinaware and porcelain not marked to indicate the country of origin at the time of importation may be released when marked by means of a gummed label or with a rubber stamp.

The Treasury Department further ruled that as of October 1, 1921, Nippon was a Japanese word (the English equivalent of which was Japan) and from that date on, all items now had to be marked Japan. Since Nippon is not considered the English name of a country, at the present time the fake backstamps under the glaze or just those stamped Nippon are allowed when a paper label is affixed indicating the country of origin. If the item is made in China and has a label attesting to this fact, the piece is allowed into the United States. The mark under the glaze has no bearing with the importation ruling.

After purchase, the paper label is easily removed and magically we now have a "Nippon" marked item.

Until recently, all the fake marks have been knock-offs of old Noritake Company backstamps. I am aware of 12 fake backstamps to date. They look something like the real thing, but not quite as good. But now they have it perfect. There is an M-in-wreath mark indistinguishable from the genuine one.

How do you tell if an item is fake or not? One tip-off is when you find items at antique shops and shows far below the market price. Beware. It's always possible, but this may be a clue that the item is not genuine. Or you suddenly see a number of pieces in the same pattern in any one shop, booth, or auction. Be extra careful when you start seeing the exact same item time after time when you are out shopping. Seasoned Nippon collectors know this does not happen. Many of the fake pieces are not hand-painted as most Nippon era wares are. They feel rougher to the touch, the gold is more of a luster color, and the glazing on some of the Chinese pieces doesn't even extend into the whole interior.

What can you do to avoid being ripped off? Get to know your Nippon or anything else you decide to collect. Buy from reputable dealers and ask for written guarantees that these are really Nippon era pieces. If in doubt, don't buy.

Before starting a collection of Nippon porcelain, collectors should buy all the books in this series and really read the text and look at all the photos. Thousands of items are shown, both real and fake. Join the International Nippon Collectors Club (INCC) for more information. Attend the annual convention where there are seminars on fake pieces. Network with other collectors and share your information on suspected pieces. Subscribe to antique trade papers. It's better to invest $25 – $75 on research information than to waste it all on a fake piece that is worthless as far as collectors are concerned. If possible, handle and touch the reproductions. Many are easily spotted but some take more time and can present a problem until collectors learn their way around.

The fakes are looking better and better and now that there is an identical mark to the M-in-wreath backstamp, it is more difficult than ever. Remember the reproduction pieces are not as light in weight (generally) and as delicate as Nippon era wares but that could change in the future. Knowledge is power. Collectors need to be on the lookout for these items and they need to be informed about what is fake. Study the photos and get to know what the reproductions look like.

Genuine items.

Items known to exist in this pattern: candlesticks, two different shaped hatpin holders, powder box, hair receiver, dresser tray, 8" tray, 8" jardiniere, 10" jardiniere, 14" jardiniere, two large bowls, and sugar shaker.

| **Genuine Backstamps** | **Fake Backstamps** | | |

Original M-in-wreath mark.

M-in-wreath
No stem.

Hourglass in an upside down wreath.

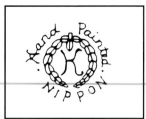

K in an upside down wreath.

M-in-wreath (blurred) Chinese mark.

M-in-wreath, word Nippon is straight across Chinese mark.

Plus, now the manufacturers in China have reproduced the M-in-wreath mark faithfully.

Genuine rising sun mark.

Japanese mark.

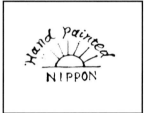

Chinese mark.

Genuine maple leaf mark. Original ¼" leaf.

Fake ½" leaf.

Genuine RC mark.

Fake RC mark.

The words "hand painted" on original mark are in red, the rest is in green. Fake mark is all green.

Genuine Backstamps   **Fake Backstamps**

Genuine komaru mark.

Fake komaru mark.

On the genuine spoke or komaru, "hand painted" is straight across.

Genuine cherry blossom mark.

Fake mark.

NIPPON

Stamped or incised on reproduction dolls or small figural items.

Large floral vase, pattern name unknown.

4" hatpin holder, egg.

Large scenic vase.

10" vase, pattern name unknown.

Two vases and tankard, antique red rose pattern.

Large hinged dresser box, pattern name unknown.

Oriental garden scene, covered urn.

Oriental garden scene, vase.

Oriental garden scene, reticulated (pierced) bowl.

Oriental garden scene,
covered bottle.

Oriental garden scene, hair receiver.

Oriental garden scene, tray, heart box, and hair receiver.

Oriental garden scene, hatpin holder.

Oriental garden scene, rolling pin, openings on each end for wooden handles.

Also known in this pattern, two vases and small reticulated bowl.

Oriental garden scene, tray, two hatpin holders.

Oriental scene, tray.

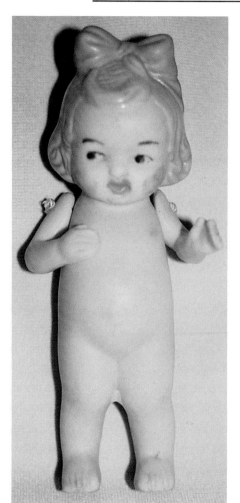

Fake dolls.

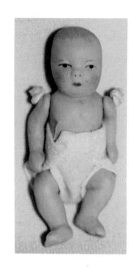

Two-piece hair receiver.

Small bowl, hair receiver.

93

Sugar shaker, vase, hatpin holder.

Small tray.

Two-piece covered dish, reticulated (pierced)
decoration.

Black mammy toothpick holder (back and front); black boy on alligator figural.

After-dinner set, comes with six cups and saucers, pattern name unknown.

Oyster dish.

Three-piece tea set, orchid pattern.

Hatpin holder.

Hair receiver.

Hair receiver.

Dogwood pattern, five-piece chocolate or mocha set, dresser set, oval box, footed bowl, heart box, berry set, trinket box, tea warmer, biscuit jar.

Pink luster pattern, hatpin holder, four chocolate sets.

Antique rose pattern, creamer and sugar bowl, two sizes of cream pitchers, night set, salt and pepper, flask, vase, tankard, and coffee set.

Wildflower pattern, four chocolate sets, urn, dresser jar, egg box, tea strainer, candlestick, lemonade set, footed box, hinged powder box, trinket box, butter dish, letter valet, bell, two dresser sets, sauce tureen, berry set, shaving mug, slanted cheese, shell dish, chamberstick, sugar bowl and creamer, bathroom set, oval box, powder dish.

Green mist pattern, sugar bowl and creamer, powder box, master sugar bowl, crimped sugar bowl, tea set.

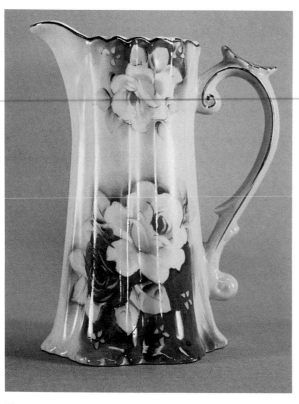

Other Texas Rose pattern, ewer.

Texas rose pattern, night set, ewer, cream pitcher, cup and saucer, tea set.

American beauty pattern, coffee set, set comes with four cups and saucers.

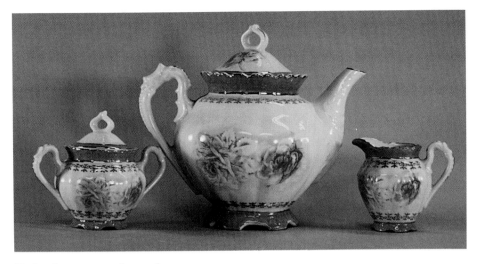

Pink mist pattern, three-piece tea set.

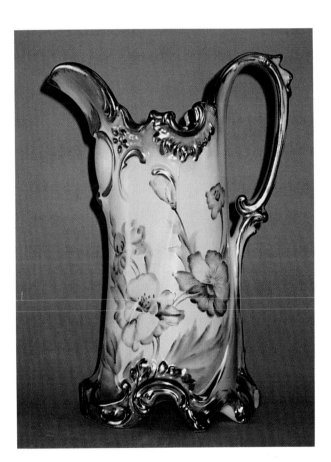

Antique spring song pattern, tankard.

Antique bouquet pattern, tankard.

Chantilly rose pattern, four tea sets, shaving mug, three hatpin holders.

Shaving mugs, first pattern name unknown; second pattern name unknown; third, beige Chantilly pattern, also available in three hatpin holders. There is a fourth shaving mug available in the Wildflower pattern.

Pattern name unknown, 6" hatpin holder, jardiniere, 8" vase, 18" umbrella stand.

Pattern name unknown, 14" vase with doll-shaped handles, 6" hatpin holder, 10" vase, 10" candlestick.

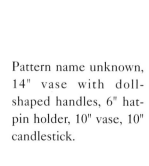

Pattern name unknown, 4" bowl, 4" hatpin holder, and small heart-shaped hair receiver, 10" candlestick.

Pattern name unknown, 10" candlestick.

Wall plaque.

Pattern name unknown, two vases, 6" hatpin holder.

Pattern name unknown, 14" vase.

Pattern name unknown, vase, 4"
hatpin holder, egg.

Pattern name unknown, 7½" vase.

Pattern name unknown, two 12" vases, 10" vase, 4" hatpin
holder.

BABY BUD NIPPON

1. Baby Bud Nippon; incised on doll.

2. Bara hand painted Nippon.

3. The Carpathia M Nippon.

4. Cherry blossom hand painted Nippon; found in blue, green, and magenta colors.

5. Cherry blossom in a circle hand painted Nippon.

6. Chikusa hand painted Nippon.

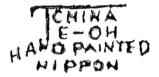

7. China E-OH hand painted Nippon; found in blue and green colors.

8. Crown (pointed), hand painted Nippon; found in green and blue colors.

9. Crown Nippon (pointed) made in Nippon; found in green and blue colors.

10. Crown (square), hand painted Nippon; found in green and green with red colors.

11. Chubby LW & Co. Nippon; found on dolls. (Louis Wolf & Co.)

15. Double T Diamond in circle Nippon.

NIPPON

D

12. D Nippon.

16. Dowsie Nippon.

13. Dolly sticker found on Nippon's Dolly dolls; sold by Morimura Bros.

17. EE Nippon.

14. Double T Diamond Nippon.

18. Elite B hand painted Nippon.

19. FY 401 Nippon;
found on dolls.

20. FY 405 Nippon;
found on dolls.

21. G in a circle hand
painted Nippon.

22. Gloria L.W. & Co. hand painted Nippon
(Louis Wolf Co., Boston, Mass. & N.Y.C.).

23. Hand painted Nippon.

Hand Painted
Nippon

24. Hand painted Nippon.

HAND PAINTED
NIPPON

25. Hand painted Nippon.

26. Hand painted Nippon.

Handpainted
NIPPON

27. Hand painted Nippon.

28. Hand painted Nippon with symbol.

33. Hand painted Nippon with symbol.

29. Hand painted Nippon with symbol.

30. Hand painted Nippon with symbol.

34. Hand painted Nippon with symbol.

31. Hand painted Nippon with symbol.

35. Hand painted Nippon with symbol.

32. Hand painted Nippon with symbol.

36. Horsman No. 1 Nippon; found on dolls.

37. IC Nippon.

38. Imperial Nippon; found in blue and green.

39. J.M.D.S. Nippon.

40. The Jonroth Studio hand painted Nippon.

41. Kid Doll M.W. & Co. Nippon.

42. Kinjo Nippon.

43. Kinjo China hand painted Nippon.

L & CO
NIPPON

44. L & Co Nippon.

45. L.F.H. hand painted Nippon.

L.W & Co.
NIPPON

46. L.W. & Co. Nippon (Louis Wolf & Co., Boston, Mass & N.Y.C.).

47. M-in-wreath, hand painted Nippon (M stands for importer, Morimura Bros.); found in green, blue, magenta & gold colors. Mark used since 1911.

51. Made in Nippon.

THE D.M. READ CO.
BRIDGEPORT, CONN.

48. M-in-wreath hand painted Nippon, D.M. Read Co. (M stands for importer, Morimura Bros.).

49. M B (Morimura Bros.) Baby Darling sticker; found on dolls.

52. Maple leaf Nippon; found in green, blue, and magenta, dates back to 1891.

53. Morimura Bros. sticker; found on Nippon items.

54. Mt. Fujiyama hand painted Nippon.

NIPPON

55. Nippon; found in blue, gold, and also incised into items.

NIPPON 84

56. Nippon 84.

NIPPON 144

57. Nippon 144.

221 NIPPON

58. Nippon 221.

59. Nippon with symbol.

60. Nippon with symbol.

61. Nippon with symbol.

NIPPON

62. Nippon with symbol.

63. Nippon with symbol.

64. Nippon with symbol.

65. Nippon M incised on doll (note N is written backwards); #12 denotes size of doll; M is Morimura Bros.

109

66. Noritake M-in-wreath Nippon; M is Morimura Bros., found in green, blue, and magenta.

67. Noritake Nippon; found in green, blue, and magenta colors.

68. Noritake Nippo; found in green, blue, and magenta colors. Mark dates from 1911, used on blank pieces (undecorated) of Nippon.

69. O.A.C. Hand painted Nippon (Okura Art China, branch of Noritake Co.).

70. Oriental china Nippon.

71. Pagoda hand painted Nippon.

PATENT
NO 30441
NIPPON

72. Patent No. 30441 Nippon.

73. Paulownia flowers and leaves hand painted Nippon (crest used by Empress of Japan, kiri no mon); found in a green/red color.

74. Paulownia flowers and leaves, hand painted Nippon (crest used by Empress of Japan, kiri no mon).

75. Pickard etched china, Noritake .Nippon.; Pickard mark is in black; Noritake/Nippon mark is blue in color.

78. Queue San Baby Sticker; found on Nippon dolls.

79. RC Nippon; RC stands for Royal Crockery (fine china).

76. W.A. Pickard hand painted china Nippon.

80. RC hand painted Nippon combination of both red and green colors. RC stands for Royal Crockery (fine china). Mark used since 1911.

81. RC Noritake Nippon hand painted; found in green and blue. RC stands for Royal Crockery (fine china). This mark has been in existence since 1911.

77. W.A. Pickard hand painted china, Noritake Nippon; Pickard mark printed in black, Noritake Nippon in magenta.

82. RC Noritake Nippon, registered in 1911. RC stands for Royal Crockery (fine china).

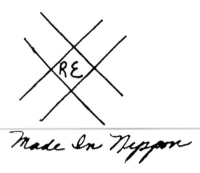

83. RE Nippon.

87. Royal Kaga Nippon.

84. Rising Sun Nippon; mark used since 1911.

88. Royal Kinran Nippon; found in blue, gold colors, made for domestic market in Japan since 1906.

85. Royal dragon Nippon.

89. Royal Kinran Crown Nippon; found in blue, gold, and green colors, made for domestic market in Japan since 1906.

90. Royal Moriye Nippon; found in green and blue colors.

86. Royal dragon Nippon studio hand painted.

91. Royal Nishiki Nippon; made for domestic market in Japan since 1906.

92. Royal Satsuma Nippon (cross within a ring, crest of House of Satsuma); made for domestic market in Japan since 1906.

93. Royal Sometuke Nippon; made for domestic market in Japan since 1906.

94. Royal Sometuke Nippon Sicily.

95. RS Nippon; found on coralene pieces.

96. S & K hand painted Nippon; found in green, blue, and magenta colors.

97. S & K hand painted Nippon; found in green, blue, and magenta colors.

98. Shinzo Nippon.

99. Shofu Nagoya Nippon.

100. SNB Nippon.

104. Studio hand painted Nippon.

101. SNB Nagoya Nippon.

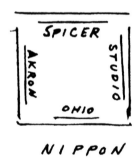

102. Spicer Studio Akron Ohio Nippon.

105. Superior hand painted Nippon.

103. Spoke hand painted Nippon;
mark in existence as early as 1911.

106. T Nippon hand painted (2 ho-o birds).

107. T hand painted Nippon.

111. TS hand painted Nippon.

108. T-in-wreath hand painted Nippon.

112. Teacup, Made in Nippon.

109. T N hand painted Nippon; mark is red and green.

113. Torii hand painted Nippon.

110. T.S. hand painted Nippon.

114. Tree crest hand painted Nippon (Crest of Morimura family); also called Spider Mark.

117. The Yamato hand painted Nippon.

115. Tree crest (also called Spider Mark) and maple leaf hand painted Nippon.

118. The Yamato Nippon.

116. V Nippon, Scranton, PA.

119. C.G.N. hand painted Nippon; found in green.

120. F Nippon 03601 600; found incised on dolls.

121. F Nippon No. 76012 601; found incised on dolls.

NO. 76018
NIPPON
30/3

122. F Nippon No. 76018
30/3; found incised on dolls.

NO. 76018
NIPPON
403

123. F Nippon No. 76018 403.

NIPPON

124. FY Nippon; found
incised on dolls.

NIPPON
301

125. FY Nippon 301; found
incised on dolls.

NIPPON
402

126. FY Nippon 402; found
incised on dolls.

NIPPON
402

127. FY 9 Nippon 402;
found incised on dolls.

NIPPON
404

128. FY Nippon 404; found
incised on dolls.

NIPPON
406

129. FY Nippon 406; found
incised on dolls.

NIPPON
464

130. FY Nippon 464; found
incised on dolls.

131. FY Nippon No. 17604 604; found incised on dolls.

132. FY Nippon No. 70018 004; found incised on dolls.

133. FY Nippon (variation of mark) No. 70018 403; found incised on dolls.

134. FY Nippon No. 70018 406; found incised on dolls.

135. FY Nippon (variation of mark) No. 70018 406; found incised on dolls.

136. FY Nippon No. 76018; found incised on dolls.

137. Jollikid Nippon sticker (red and white); found on dolls.

138. Ladykin Nippon sticker (red & gold); found on dolls.

139. Nippon (notice reversal of first N); found incised on items.

NIPPON
D13495

140. Nippon D13495; found in green.

NIPPON
E

141. Nippon E; found incised on dolls.

O
NIPPON

142. Nippon O; found incised on dolls.

5
NIPPON

143. Nippon 5; found incised on dolls.

97
NIPPON

144. Nippon 97; found incised on dolls.

98
NIPPON

145. Nippon 98; found incised on dolls.

99
NIPPON

146. Nippon 99; found incised on dolls.

101
NIPPON

147. Nippon 101; found incised on dolls.

102
NIPPON

148. Nippon 102; found incised on dolls.

149. Nippon 105; found incised on dolls.

150. Nippon 123; found incised on dolls.

151. Nippon 144 with symbol; found incised on dolls.

152. RE Nippon.

153. RE made in Nippon; found incised on dolls.

154. RE Nippon A9; found incised on dolls.

155. RE Nippon B8; found incised on dolls.

156. RE Nippon O 2; found incised on dolls.

157. Royal Hinode Nippon; found in blue.

158. Sonny sticker (gold, red, white, and blue); found on dolls.

159. Maruta Royal Blue Nippon.

160. Hand Painted Coronation Ware Nippon.

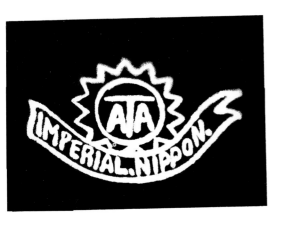

161. ATA Imperial Nippon.

162. Baby Doll, M.W. & Co. Nippon sticker; found on dolls.

163. BE, 4 Nippon.

164. Cherry blossom Nippon, similar to No. 4.

165. Cherry blossom (double) Nippon.

166. C O L Nippon.

167. C.O.N. Hand Painted Nippon.

168. FY Nippon 405.

169. FY Nippon 505.

170. FY Nippon 601.

171. FY Nippon 602.

172. FY Nippon 1602.

173. FY Nippon 603 NO. 76018.

174. Happifat Nippon sticker; found on dolls.

175. H in circle Nippon.

176. Horsman Nippon, B9.

177. James Studio China logo; used in conjunction with Crown Nippon mark.

178. JPL Hand Painted Nippon.

179. Kenilworth Studios Nippon.

180. Komaru symbol, Hand Painted Nippon, since 1912.

181. Komaru symbol, Hand Painted Nippon No. 16034. Note: Japanese characters are fictitious.

182. M Nippon 10.

183. M Nippon F24.

184. Manikin Nippon sticker; found on dolls.

185. Meiyo China Y-in-circle Nippon.

NIPPON
3

186. Nippon 3.

A3
NIPPON

187. Nippon A3.

188. Nippon 144.

189. Nippon with symbol.

190. Nippon with symbol.

191. Nippon with symbol.

192. Nippon with symbol.

193. Nippon with symbol.

194. Nippon with symbol.

195. Nippon with symbol.

196. Nippon with symbol.

197. Hand painted Nippon with symbol.

198. Nippon with symbol, H in diamond, 14 B, P. 4.

199. Noritake M-in-wreath Nippon; M is Morimura Bros.; found in green, blue, and magenta; Derby indicates pattern.

200. Noritake M-in-wreath Nippon; M is Morimura Bros.; Sahara indicates pattern.

201. Noritake M-in-wreath Nippon; M is Morimura Bros.; The Kiva indicates pattern.

202. Noritake M-in-wreath Nippon; M is Morimura Bros.; The Metz indicates pattern.

203. Noritake M-in-wreath Nippon; M is Morimura Bros. Registered in Japan in 1912.

204. Noritake M-in-wreath Hand Painted Nippon; M is Morimura Bros.; Marguerite indicates pattern.

205. Noritake M-in-wreath Hand Painted Nippon; M is Morimura Bros.; Sedan indicates pattern. First dinner set made in Noritake factory 1914.

THE VITRY

WAVERLY

NPMC
NIPPON
HAND PAINTED

206. Noritake M-in-wreath Hand Painted Nippon; M is Morimura Bros.; The Vitry indicates pattern.

207. NPMC Nippon Hand Painted.

208. RC Noritake Nippon; Waverly indicates pattern.

209. RE Nippon 1120.

210. RE Nippon 04.

211. RE Nippon B 9.

212. RE Made in Nippon A4.

213. RE Made in Nippon A5.

214. RE Made in Nippon B9.

215. RE Made in Nippon B1001.

216. Royal Kuyu Nippon.

217. S in circle Nippon.

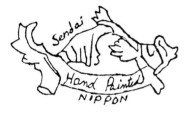

218. Sendai Hand Painted Nippon.

219. Stouffer Hand Painted Nippon.

220. Tanega Hand Painted Nippon.

221. Torii Nippon; similar to No. 113.

222. Nagoya N & Co. Nippon.

223. Old Blue Nippon Hand Painted.

* These marks were used during the Nippon era but may have also been used after 1921.

224.* RC Noritake mark, used for domestic market in Japan by Noritake Co. since 1908. The RC stands for Royal Crockery (fine china). The symbol design is called Yajirobe (toy of balance). It symbolizes the balance in management.

225.* RC Noritake mark, used for domestic market in Japan by Noritake Co. since 1912. The RC stands for Royal Crockery (fine china). The symbol design is called Yajirobe (toy of balance). It symbolizes the balance in management.

226.* RC Nippontoki-Nagoya mark, for export since 1911. The RC stands for Royal Crockery (fine china).

227.* Made in Japan mark, used by Noritake Co., registered in London in 1908.

228.* Noritaké, made in Japan, for export to England, registered in 1908 by Noritake Co.

229.* Noritaké, registered in London in 1908 by Noritake Co.

230.* Noritake, made in Japan mark, registered in London in 1908.

231.* RC Japan; Noritake Co. started using the mark in 1914. It was used on items sent to India and Southeast Asia. RC stands for Royal Crockery (fine china).

232 Coalportia Nippon.

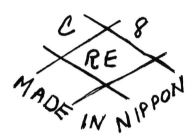

236. No. 700 Nippon HO6;
found incised on dolls.

233. FY Nippon 302; found
incised on dolls.

237. RE Made in Nippon C8;
found incised on dolls.

234. FY Nippon 303; found
incised on dolls.

238. RE Nippon, M18; found
incised on dolls.

235. FY Nippon 501; found
incised on dolls.

239. SK Hand Painted Made in Nippon.

240. Patent No. 17705 Royal Kinjo.

244. Kinran U.S. Patent 912171; found on coralene pieces.

247. FY Nippon 204; found on dolls.

241. RS Japan; found on coralene pieces.

245. Patent applied for No. 38257; found on coralene pieces.

248. FY Nippon 409; found on dolls.

242. U.S. Patent 912171; found on coralene pieces.

243. U.S. Patent 912171; found on coralene pieces.

246. Kinran Patent No. 16137; found on coralene pieces.

249. FY Nippon 15/4; found on dolls.

130

250. ESO hand-paint-
ed Nippon.

251. Miyako Nippon.

252. Royal Fuji Nippon.

253. RC Noritake, Nippon
Toki Kaisha, circa 1912.

254. Komaru Nippon, circa 1906.

255. Noritake Howo, circa 1916.

256. Chikaramachi, made in
Japan, circa 1912.

257. Noritake M, Japan, circa 1916.

258. Kokura, Japan, circa 1920.

FY

No. 76018
NIPPON
402

259. FY Nippon No. 76018, 402
found incised on dolls.

FY

NIPPON
11148

260. FY Nippon, 11148, found
incised on dolls.

COBALT

Plate 2907. Vase, 6¾" tall, blue mark #52, $400.00 – 475.00.

Plate 2908. Ewer, 7½" tall, blue mark #52, $435.00 – 500.00.

Plate 2909. Vase, 13½" tall, blue mark #52, $950.00 – 1,100.00.

Plate 2910. Vase, 12" tall, green mark #52, $700.00 – 800.00.

Plate 2911. Vase, 5½" tall, blue mark #47, $400.00 – 500.00.

Plate 2912. Vase, 9" tall, blue mark #52, $500.00 – 600.00.

Plate 2913. Vase, cobalt with heavy gold overlay, 12¼" tall, blue mark #52, $700.00 – 800.00.

Plate 2914. Vase, 10" tall, blue mark #52, $800.00 – 950.00.

Plate 2915. Vase, 7" tall, mark #42, $400.00 – 500.00.

Plate 2916. Vase, 8¾" tall, blue mark #38, $500.00 – 600.00.

Plate 2918. Vase, 7" tall, blue mark #52, $400.00 – 500.00.

Plate 2917. Ewer, 10½" tall, unmarked, $500.00 – 600.00.

Plate 2919. Vase, 10" tall, blue mark #52, $400.00 – 500.00. Ewer, 7" tall, blue mark #52, $400.00 – 500.00.

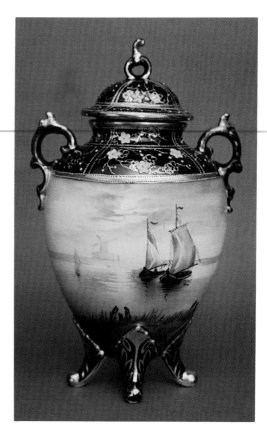

Plate 2920. Covered urn, 8¾" tall, green mark #47, $650.00 – 750.00.

Plate 2921. Covered urn, 9½" tall, unmarked, $550.00 – 650.00.

Plate 2922. Bolted urn, 16" tall, green mark #47, $2,500.00 – 3,000.00.

Plate 2923. Punch bowl and base, 10" across, blue mark #52, $550.00 – 650.00.

Plate 2924. Bolted urn, 12" tall, mark #88, $900.00 – 1,100.00.

Plate 2925. Vase, 23½" tall, blue mark #47, $3,000.00 – 3,500.00.

Plate 2926. Plate, 10" wide, green mark #47, $300.00 – 400.00.

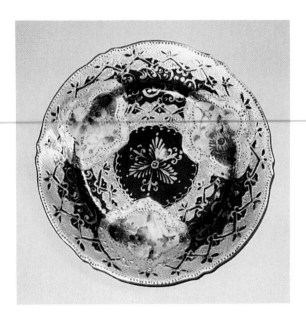

Plate 2927. Cake plate, 6" wide, blue mark #52, $65.00 – 80.00.

Plate 2928. Ferner, 8" in diameter, green mark #47, $400.00 – 500.00.

Plate 2929. Pair of vases, 16" tall, mark #38, 1,800.00 – 2,400.00 pr.

Plate 2930. Tea set, green mark #47, $850.00 – 1,000.00.

Plate 2931. Bouillon cup and underplate, unmarked, $160.00 – 200.00.

Plate 2932. Cookie/cracker jar, 8" tall, blue mark #52, $500.00 – 600.00.

Plate 2933. Demitasse pot with four cups and saucers, green mark #47, $400.00 – 550.00.

Plate 2934. Luncheon set, consists of ten 8¾" wide plates, ten cake plates, 6¼" wide, and a creamer and sugar bowl, mark #81, $400.00 – 500.00.

Plate 2935. Berry bowl set, master bowl is 11" wide, set contains six bowls which are 5¼" wide, mark #47, $600.00 – 700.00.

Plate 2936. Chocolate set, pot is 10½" tall, blue mark #52, $800.00 – 900.00.

Plate 2937. Dish, 7" wide, blue mark #52, $125.00 – 140.00.

Plate 2938. Bowl, 4½" wide, blue mark #52, $450.00 – 550.00.

Plate 2939. Ramekin, underplate is 5¼" wide, green mark #52, $125.00 – 160.00.

Plate 2940. Covered dish, 6" wide, mark #47, $225.00 – 300.00.

Plate 2941. Nut set, master bowl is 7½" wide, green mark #47, $300.00 – 375.00.

Plate 2942. Nut set, master bowl is 7½" wide, green mark #47, $325.00 – 400.00.

Plate 2943. Dresser set, unmarked, $1,200.00 – 1,400.00.

Plate 2944. Cookie/cracker jar, 7¾" tall, blue mark #52, $500.00 – 600.00

Plate 2945. Tankard, 16½" tall, blue mark #52, $900.00 – 1,000.00.

PORTRAIT

Plate 2946. Vase, 7" tall, green mark #52, $1,000.00 – 1,200.00. Vase, 7½" tall, green mark #52, $1,000.00 – 1,200.00.

Plate 2947. Vase, 12" tall, blue mark #52, $1,300.00 – 1,500.00.

Plate 2948. Vase, 6½" tall, blue mark #52, $1,000.00 – 1,200.00.

Plate 2949. Vase, 8½" tall, green mark #52, $1,100.00 – 1,250.00.
Ewer, 9" tall, green mark #52, $1,200.00 – 1,350.00.

Plate 2950. Vase, 9" tall, blue mark #52,
$1,200.00 – 1,350.00.

Plate 2952. Vase, 7" tall, green mark #47,
$1,000.00 – 1,200.00.

Plate 2951. Vase, 7¾" tall, green
mark #52, $1,000.00 – 1,200.00.

Plate 2953. Vase, 7¾" tall, green mark #52, $1,000.00 – 1,200.00.

Plate 2954. Covered urn, 14" tall, blue mark #52, $2,000.00 – 2,400.00.

Plate 2955. Bolted covered urn, 14" tall, blue mark #52, $2,500.00 – 3,000.00.

Plate 2956. Covered urn (back view of Plate 2955).

Plate 2957. Covered urn, 25½" tall, mark has been removed, $4,000.00 – 5,000.00.

Plate 2958. Vase, 16" tall, blue mark #52, $1,700.00 – 2,000.00.

Plate 2959. Covered urn, 33" tall, unmarked, $5,000.00 – 6,500.00.

Plate 2960. Vase (Lady with Doves), 8" tall, green mark #52, $900.00 – 1,100.00. Vase, (Lady with Doves), 9¼" tall, blue mark #52, $1,000.00 – 1,200.00.

Plate 2961. Ewer, 5" tall, mark #52, $700.00 – 850.00.

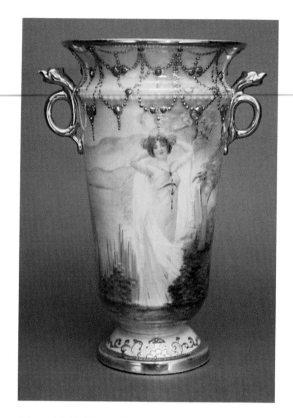

Plate 2962. Vase (Lady with Peacock), 8" tall, green mark #52, $950.00 – 1,100.00.

Plate 2963. Vase (Lebrun), 9½" tall, unmarked, $1,000.00 – 1,200.00.

Plate 2964. Vase, 5½" tall, blue mark #52, $800.00 – 900.00.

Plate 2965. Vase, 8" tall, green mark #52, $900.00 – 1,100.00.

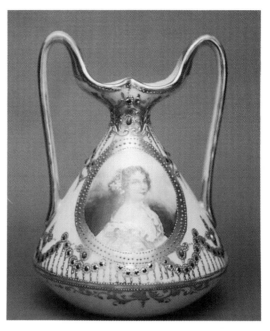

Plate 2966. Vase, 7" tall, blue mark #52, $850.00 – 1,000.00.

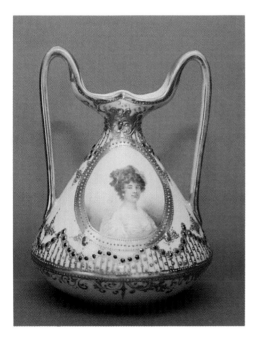

Plate 2967. Vase, 7" tall, blue mark #52, $850.00 – 1,000.00.

Plate 2968. Vase, 9" tall, green #47, $1,000.00 – 1,200.00.

Plate 2970. Cookie/cracker jar, 6" tall, green mark #52, $800.00 – 1,000.00. Ewer, 6" tall, green mark #52, $800.00 – 1,000.00.

Plate 2969. Covered urn, 10½" tall, blue mark #52, $1,300.00 – 1,500.00.

Plate 2971. Plate (The Cardinal), 6¾" wide, blue mark #52, $800.00 – 1,000.00.

Plate 2972. Mug (The Cardinal), 5½" tall, $800.00 – 1,000.00.

Plate 2973. Vase (Queen Victoria), 6" tall, part of mark is scratched off, word Nippon is still visible, $700.00 – 900.00.

Plate 2974. Vase, 8½" tall, blue mark #52, $1,000.00 – 1,200.00

Plate 2975. Humidor, 8" tall, blue mark #52, $2,000.00 – 2,400.00.

Plate 2976. Plate, 8¾" wide, blue mark #52, $1,000.00 – 1,200.00.

Plate 2977. Hanging plaque, 9¾" wide, blue mark #52, $1,000.00 – 1,200.00.

Plate 2978. Covered box, 5½" wide, blue mark #52, $700.00 – 850.00.

Plate 2979. Hanging plaque, 10" wide, green mark #52, $950.00 – 1,150.00.

Plate 2980. Two-piece egg, 5½" long, unmarked, $750.00 – 900.00.

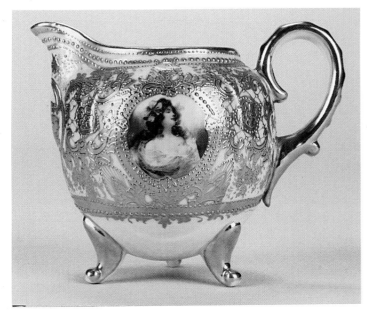

Plate 2981. Creamer, 4¼" tall, green mark #52, $350.00 – 400.00.

Plate 2982. Vase, 6½" tall, unmarked, $800.00 – 950.00.

Plate 2983. Teapot, 6½" tall, blue mark #52, $625.00 – 725.00.

Plate 2984. Gravy boat, mark #52, $500.00 – 625.00.

Plate 2985. Cologne bottle, blue mark #52, $525.00 – 650.00.

Plate 2986. Bowl, 7¾" long, green mark #52, $525.00 – 650.00.

TAPESTRY

Plate 2987. Vase, 8" tall, blue mark #52, $900.00 – 1,100.00. Vase, 6½" tall, blue mark #52, $750.00 – 900.00.

Plate 2988. Vase, 7½" tall, green mark #52, $850.00 – 1,000.00.

Plate 2989. Vase, 3" tall, blue mark #52, $450.00 – 525.00.

Plate 2990. Vase, 7¼" tall, blue mark #52, $800.00 – 1,000.00.

Plate 2991. Vase, 8½" tall, green mark #52, $900.00 – 1,100.00.

Plate 2992. Ewer, 7" tall, blue mark #52, $850.00 – 1,000.00.

Plate 2993. Ewer, 7" tall, blue mark #52, $850.00 – 1,000.00.

Plate 2994. Pitcher, 6¼" tall, green mark #47, $700.00 – 800.00.

Plate 2995. Humidor, 6" tall, blue mark #52, $1,800.00 – 2,200.00.

Plate 2996. Vase, 9½" tall, blue mark #4, $750.00 – 850.00.

HEAVILY BEADED VASES

Plate 2997. Cloisonne vase, 6" tall, green mark #47, $425.00 – 500.00.

Plate 2998. Vase, 7½" tall, blue mark #52, $450.00 – 550.00.

Plate 3000. Vase, 5" tall, green mark #52, $400.00 – 500.00.

Plate 2999. Vase, 9½" tall, blue mark #52, $500.00 – 600.00. Ewer, 7" tall, blue mark #52, $400.00 – 500.00.

Plate 3001. Vase, 10" tall, unmarked, $600.00 – 700.00.

Plate 3002. Demitasse set, pot is 9" tall, blue mark #52, $1,100.00 – 1,300.00.

Plate 3003. Vase, 4½" tall, green mark #52, $250.00 – 350.00. Vase, 4½" tall, blue mark #52, $250.00 – 350.00.

Plate 3004. Vase, 4¾" tall, mark #90, $350.00 – 450.00.

Plate 3005. Compote/loving cup, 5" tall, green mark #47, $550.00 – 650.00.

Plate 3006. Flower gate, 7" long, mark #47, $500.00 – 600.00.

WEDGWOOD

Plate 3007. Cheese dish, tray is 7¾" long, green mark #47, $450.00 – 550.00.

Plate 3008. Vase, 9½" tall, green mark #47, $600.00 – 700.00.

Plate 3009. Ashtray, 5"
tall, green mark #47,
$750.00 – 850.00.

Plate 3010. Smoke
set, tray is 10" long,
green mark #47,
$900.00 – 1,100.00.

Plate 3011. Lavender orchid bowl, 8¼" wide, green mark #47,
$650.00 — 750.00

Plate 3012. Potpourri jar, green mark #47, $400.00 –
500.00.

Plate 3013. Bowl, 7" tall, green mark #47, $275.00 – 350.00.

Plate 3014. Vase, gold overlay, 12¾" tall, green mark #47, $1,000.00 – 1,200.00.

MISCELLANEOUS

Plate 3015. Urn, gold overlay, 13" tall, blue mark #52, $1,700.00 – 2,000.00.

Plate 3016. Vase, gold overlay, 8½" tall, green mark #101, $600.00 – 700.00.

Plate 3017. Chocolate set, gold overlay, pot is 8¾" tall, green mark #47, $700.00 – 850.00.

Plate 3018. Hanging plaque, gold overlay, 9" diameter, green mark #47, $375.00 – 475.00.

Plate 3019. Ewer, gold overlay, 12" tall, blue mark #52, $600.00 – 700.00.

Plate 3020. Vase, sponge tapestry, 9½" tall, blue mark #52, $450.00 – 550.00.

Plate 3021. Butter dish, silver overlay, 7½" wide, magenta mark #82, $250.00 – 325.00.

Plate 3022. Vase, silver overlay, 7" tall, mark #52, $300.00 – 400.00.

Plate 3023. Condensed milk container, silver overlay, magenta mark #82, $250.00 – 325.00.

MORIAGE

Plate 3024. Vase, 5½" tall, green mark #47, $150.00 – 200.00. Vase, 5" tall, green mark #47, $150.00 – 200.00. Vase, 5½" tall, green mark #47, $150.00 – 200.00.

Plate 3025. Loving cup, 4¼" tall, green mark #47, $175.00 – 225.00. Loving cup, 5½" tall, green mark #47, $225.00 – 275.00.

Plate 3026. Vase, 5½" tall, green mark #347, $175.00 – 225.00. Vase, 6" tall, blue mark #52, $225.00 – 275.00.

Plate 3027. Humidor, 5½" tall, blue mark #52, $650.00 – 750.00.

Plate 3028. Vase, 9" tall, green mark #47, $300.00 – 375.00.

Plate 3029. Vase, 9½" tall, mark #32, $225.00 – 275.00.

Plate 3030. Vase, 4" tall, green mark #27, $250.00 – 300.00.

Plate 3031. Vase, 7½" tall, mark removed, $400.00 – 500.00.

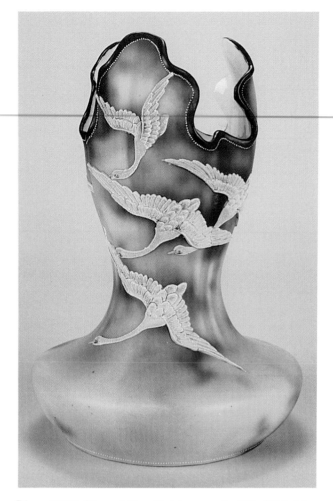

Plate 3032. Vase, 12" tall, blue mark #52, $775.00 – 875.00.

Plate 3033. Vase, 6½" tall, mark removed, $450.00 – 550.00.

Plate 3034. Vase 6½" tall, blue mark #52, $450.00 – 550.00.

Plate 3035. Vase, 8½" tall, blue mark #52, $550.00 – 650.00.

Plate 3036. Vase, 8½" tall, blue mark #70, $550.00 – 650.00.

Plate 3037. Mug, 4¾" tall, blue mark #52, $300.00 – 400.00.

Plate 3038. Vase, 9¾" tall, green mark #47, $700.00 – 850.00.

Plate 3039. Hanging plaque, 12½" wide, blue mark #52, $800.00 – 900.00.

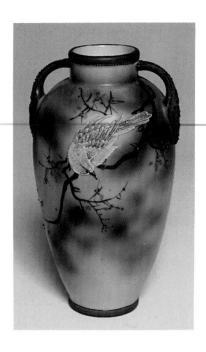

Plate 3040. Vase, 5¼"
tall, green mark #47,
$325.00 – 400.00.

Plate 3041. Humidor,
6½" tall, green mark #52,
$700.00 – 850.00.

Plate 3042. Vase, 10" tall, unmarked, $400.00 – 500.00.

Plate 3043. Vase, 10½" tall, mark #90,
$600.00 – 700.00.

Plate 3044. Pair of mirror image vases, 10½" tall, blue mark #115, $600.00 – 700.00 each.

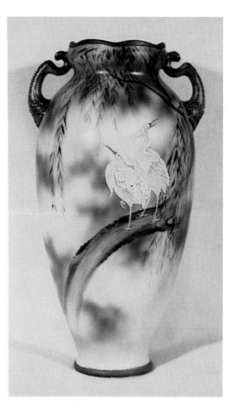

Plate 3045. Vase, 9¾" tall, green mark #47, $550.00 – 650.00.

Plate 3046. Vase, 9½" tall, blue mark #52, $550.00 – 650.00.

Plate 3047. Hanging plaque, 13¼" wide, blue mark #52, $1,500.00 – 1,700.00.

Plate 3049. Vase, 9¾" tall, blue mark #352, $650.00 – 750.00.

Plate 3048. Vase, 11½" tall, blue mark #52, $650.00 – 725.00.

Plate 3050. Bowl, 9¼" wide, unmarked, $200.00 – 300.00.

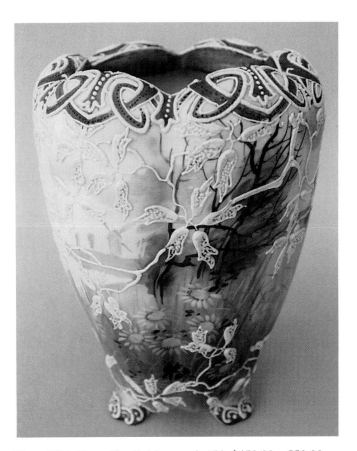

Plate 3051. Vase, 8" tall, blue mark #52, $450.00 – 550.00.

Plate 3052. Vase, 8½" tall, mark #90, $525.00 – 600.00.

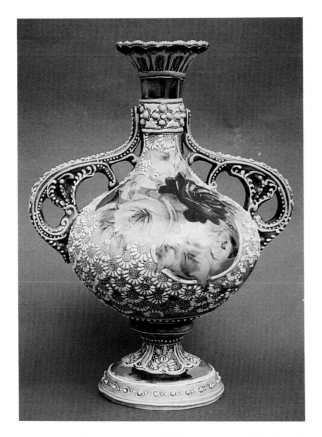

Plate 3053. Vase (bolted), 8¼" tall, mark #90, $375.00 – 450.00.

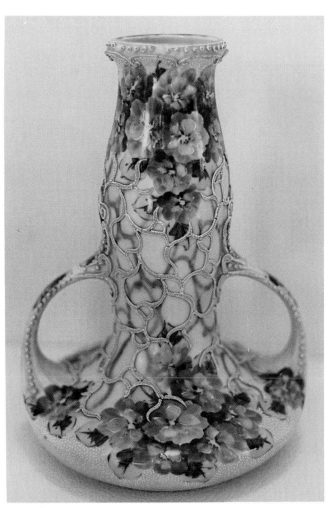

Plate 3054. Vase, 9½" tall, unmarked, $450.00 – 550.00.

Plate 3055. Humidor, 7½" tall, blue mark #52, $1,000.00 – 1,150.00.

Plate 3056. Vase, 5½" tall, blue mark #52, $400.00 – 500.00.

Plate 3057. Bolted urn, 8½" tall, unmarked, $650.00 – 750.00.

Plate 3058. Covered urn, 11" tall, mark #52, $900.00 – 1,050.00.

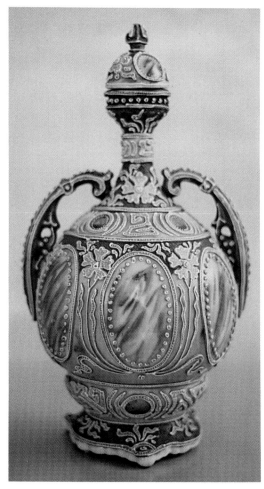

Plate 3059. Covered urn, 10" tall, unmarked, $650.00 – 750.00.

Plate 3060. Humidor, white woodland pattern, 6¾" tall, blue mark #47, $825.00 – 925.00.

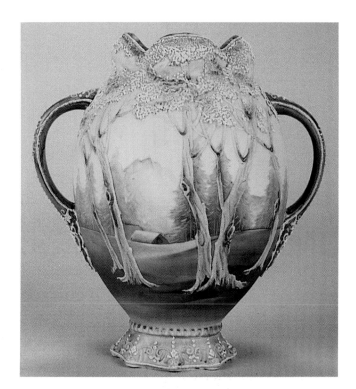

Plate 3062. Vase, white woodland pattern, 10" tall, green mark #47, $625.00 – 725.00.

Plate 3061. Pitcher, white woodland pattern, 7" tall, blue mark #47, $525.00 – 625.00.

Plate 3063. Vase, white woodland pattern, 8½" tall, green mark #47, $600.00 – 700.00.

Plate 3064. Hanging plaque, white woodland pattern, 10" wide, blue mark #47, $400.00 – 500.00.

Plate 3066. Vase, 4½" tall, blue mark #16, $275.00 – 325.00.

Plate 3065. Vase, 8¾" tall, blue mark #52, $350.00 – 400.00.

Plate 3067. Vase, 5¾" tall, unmarked, $275.00 – 325.00.

Plate 3068. Vase, 8½" tall, green mark #52, $425.00 – 475.00.

Plate 3069. Vase, 7" tall, unmarked, $325.00 – 375.00.

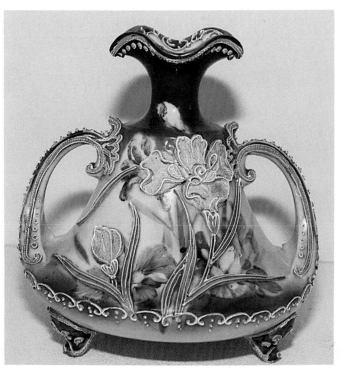

Plate 3070. Vase, 7" tall, unmarked, $325.00 – 375.00.

Plate 3072. Vase, 3¾" tall, blue mark #52, $200.00 – 250.00.

Plate 3071. Vase, 9½" tall, blue mark #52, $475.00 – 550.00.

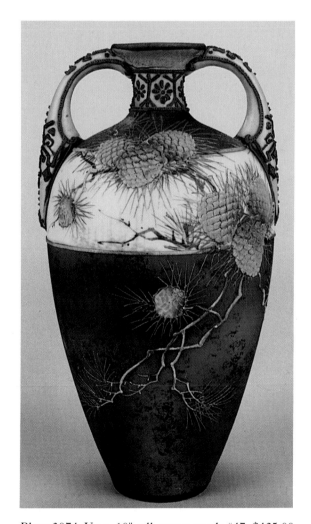

Plate 3073. Vase, 7" tall, blue mark #52, $275.00 – 325.00.

Plate 3074. Vase, 10" tall, green mark #47, $425.00 – 500.00.

Plate 3076. Vase, 5¾" tall, unmarked, $325.00 – 375.00.

Plate 3075. Vase, 8¼" tall, blue mark, #52, $400.00 – 475.00.

Plate 3077. Vase, 6½" tall, unmarked, $225.00 – 275.00.

Plate 3078. Vase, 9" tall, unmarked, $300.00 – 375.00.

Plate 3080. Vase, 9" tall, unmarked, $400.00 – 450.00.

Plate 3079. Vase, 11½" tall, green mark #47, $300.00 – 375.00.

Plate 3081. Vase, 6½" tall, blue mark #52, $500.00 – 600.00.

Plate 3082. Vase, 7½" tall, blue mark #52, $500.00 – 600.00.

Plate 3083. Vase, 10" tall, green mark #52,
$400.00 – 475.00.

Plate 3084. Vase, 2" tall, green mark #52, $200.00 – 250.00. Ewer, 7½" tall, green mark #70,
$400.00 – 450.00. Vase, 9½" tall, green mark #52, $500.00 – 600.00. Handled dish, 6¾" wide,
green mark #52, $250.00 – 300.00.

Plate 3085. Vase, 14" tall, unmarked, $750.00 – 850.00.

Plate 3086. Vase, 6" tall, blue mark #47, $300.00 – 350.00.

Plate 3087. Vase, 6" tall, unmarked, $375.00 – 450.00.

Plate 3088. Vase, 9½" tall, blue mark #52, $675.00 – 775.00.

Plate 3089. Tankard, 11¾" tall, unmarked, $550.00 – 650.00.

Plate 3090. Tankard, 10½" tall, unmarked, $650.00 – 800.00.

Plate 3091. Vase, 3" tall, unmarked, $150.00 – 200.00.

Plate 3092. Vase, 5½" tall, blue mark #52, $325.00 – 400.00.

Plate 3093. Vase, moriage with molded in relief technique, 9½" tall, green mark #47, $1,400.00 – 1,600.00.

Plate 3094. Tankard, 10½" tall, unmarked, $700.00 – 800.00.

Plate 3095. Humidor, 7½" tall, unmarked, $625.00 – 725.00.

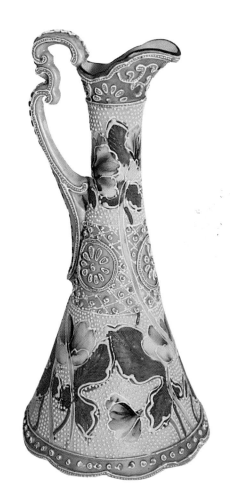

Plate 3097. Ewer,
7½" tall, unmarked,
$325.00 – 400.00.

Plate 3096. Ewer, 10½" tall, unmarked, $425.00
– 500.00.

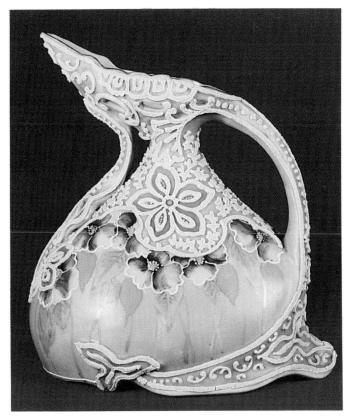

Plate 3098. Ewer, 7" tall,
unmarked, $425.00 – 500.00.

183

Plate 3099. Tankard, 16" tall, unmarked,
$900.00 – 1,100.00

Plate 3100. Chocolate pot, 10" tall,
unmarked, $375.00 – 450.00.

Plate 3101. Shaving mug, 3¼" tall, mark #90, $300.00 – 350.00. Shaving mug, 3¼" tall,
mark #90, $300.00 – 375.00.

Plate 3102. Domed match holder and striker, 3" tall, unmarked, $325.00 – 375.00.

Plate 3103. Covered jar, 6" tall, green mark #47, $300.00 – 375.00.

Plate 3104. Hanging plaque, 10" wide, blue mark #52, $300.00 – 375.00.

Plate 3105. Domed match holder and striker, 3" tall, mark #90, $400.00 – 500.00.

Plate 3106. Cookie/cracker jar, 8½" tall, unmarked, $450.00 – 525.00.

Plate 3107. Humidor, 7¾" tall, unmarked, $575.00 – 675.00.

Plate 3108. Ewer, 8" tall, mark #70, $425.00 – 500.00.

Plate 3109. Humidor, 7¾" tall, unmarked, $625.00 – 725.00.

Plate 3110. Domed match holder and striker, 3" tall, blue mark #52, $300.00 – 400.00.

RELIEF MOLDED

Plate 3111. Vase, 14¼" tall, mark #4, $500.00 – 600.00.

Plate 3112. Vase, 7¾" tall, green mark #47, $1,500.00 – 1,700.00.

Plate 3113. Vase, 8½" tall, green mark #47, $1,500.00 – 1,700.00.

Plate 3114. Vase, 10" tall, green mark #47, $1,600.00 – 1,800.00.

Plate 3115. Vase, 9½" tall, green mark #47, $500.00 – 600.00.

Plate 3117. Basket dish, 8½" tall, green mark #47, $500.00 – 600.00.

Plate 3116. Hanging plaque (similar to Plate 123), 10½" wide, green mark #47, $900.00 – 1,100.00.

Plate 3119. Ashtray, 2¾" tall, green mark #47, $675.00 – 750.00.

Plate 3118. Hanging plaque (charger), 14" wide, green mark #47, $1,400.00 – 1,600.00.

Plate 3120. Ferner, 6¾" wide, Roman figures in three panels, green mark #47, $1,200.00 – 1,400.00.

Plate 3120a. Different view of Plate 3120.

Plate 3121. Nut dish, 8" long, green mark #47, $225.00 – 300.00.

Plate 3122. Relief molded basket dish, 6" long, green mark #47, $275.00 – 350.00.

Plate 3123. Relief molded ashtray, 2½" wide, green mark #47, $500.00 – 600.00.

Plate 3124. Relief molded bowl, 9" wide, green mark #47, $450.00 – 550.00.

FIGURALS

Plate 3125. Figural ferner, 7¼" wide, blue mark #38, $300.00 – 400.00.

Plate 3126. Lamp, similar to plate #593, this piece has a factory glazed cut-out section for lamp cord, green mark #47, $1,400.00 – 1,700.00.

Plate 3126a. Back view of lamp shown in Plate 3126.

Plate 3127. Bird bowl, 7" wide, blue mark #84, $250.00 – 300.00. Figural bird dish, 6" wide, blue mark #84, $250.00 – 300.00.

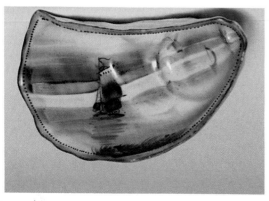

Plate 3128. Shell shaped dish, 5" long, blue mark #52, $175.00 – 225.00.

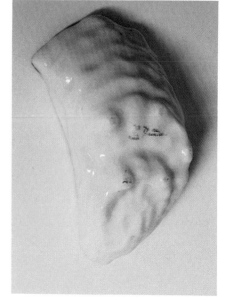

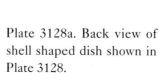

Plate 3128a. Back view of shell shaped dish shown in Plate 3128.

Plate 3129. Bird bowl, 7" wide, green mark #47, $250.00 – 300.00.

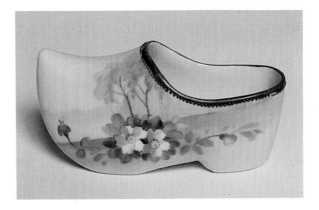

Plate 3130. Dutch shoe, 4¼" long, green mark #47, $185.00 – 235.00.

Plate 3131. Ashtray, 4½" wide, mark is indistinguishable but word Nippon is present, $400.00 – 500.00.

Plate 3132. Ashtray, similar to Plate 2592, 7" wide, green mark #47, $925.00 – 1,050.00.

Plate 3133. Ashtray, mark #84, $135.00 – 160.00.

Plate 3134. Compote/comport, similar to Plate 2589, 7½" wide, green mark #47, $475.00 – 575.00.

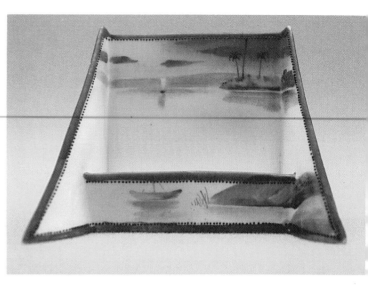

Plate 3135. Figural compote/comport 7¼" wide, green mark #47. $475.00 – 575.00.

Plate 3136. Calendar holder, 3" tall, green mark #47, advertising "Compliments of Hammond Milling Co., Seattle, U.S.A.," $225.00 – 275.00.

Plate 3137. Nipper, Souvenir of Springfield, Ill., green mark #55, $175.00 – 225.00.

Plate 3136a. Back view of Plate 3136.

SOUVENIRS

Plate 3138. Mug, 5½" tall, green mark, souvenir of Delaware Water Gap, green mark #47, $275.00 – 350.00.

Plate 3139. Dish, 7" across, blue mark #52, souvenir of Prospect Point, Niagara Falls, $90.00 – 135.00.

Plate 3140. Vase, souvenir of Capitol Building, Washington, D.C., 6½" tall, mark #90, $450.00 – 525.00. Vase, souvenir of Capitol Building, Washington, D.C., 7" tall, mark #90, $450.00 – 525.00.

Plate 3141. Pin tray, souvenir of 1000 Islands, 6¼" long, blue mark #52, $125.00 – 160.00.

Plate 3142. Toothbrush holder, souvenir of 1000 Islands, 3" tall, green mark #47, $85.00 – 135.00.

Plate 3143. Tray, souvenir of Mt. Rainier and Lake Washington, 12½" long, mark #100, $175.00 — 250.00.

Plate 3144. Cake plate, souvenir of Capitol Building, Washington, D.C., 8½" diameter, blue mark #52, $175.00 – 250.00.

Plate 3146. Ashtray, 4¼" wide, souvenir of Atlantic City, N.J., 4¼" wide, mark #84, $100.00 – 135.00.

Plate 3145. Covered jar, 6" tall, souvenir of Capitol Building, Washington, D.C., blue mark #52, $175.00 – 250.00.

Plate 3147. Dish, souvenir of Capitol Building, Washington, D.C., green mark #52, $100.00 – 135.00.

CORALENE

Plate 3149. Coralene hanging plaque, 11" diameter, mark #242, $2,200.00 – 2,700.00.

Plate 3148. Nappy, souvenir of Capitol Building, Washington, D.C., 5" wide, $100.00 – 135.00.

Plate 3150. Coralene hanging plaque, 9¾" wide, mark #242, $750.00 – 900.00.

Plate 3151. Hanging plaque, 9¾" wide, mark #242, $2,000.00 – 2,500.00.

Plate 3152. Pair of covered urns, 12½" tall, mark #242, $1,100.00 – 1,300.00 each.

Plate 3153. Covered urn, 7½" tall, mark #245, $1,200.00 – 1,500.00.

Plate 3154. Covered urn, 7¾" tall, mark #242, $1,200.00 – 1,500.00.

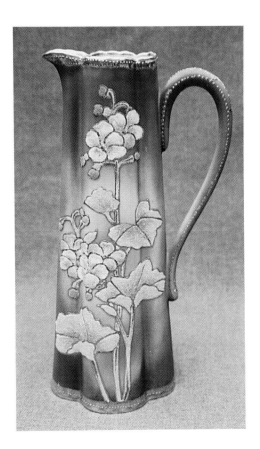

Plate 3155. Tankard, 12" tall, unmarked, $1,100.00 – 1,300.00.

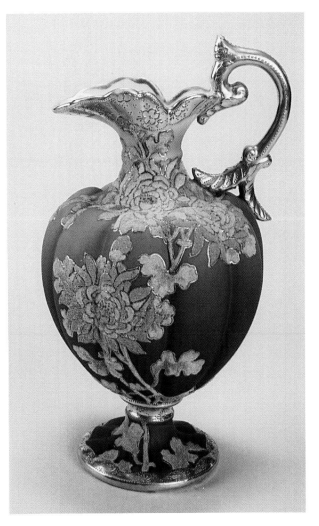

Plate 3156. Ewer, 11" tall, mark #243, $1,400.00 – 1,800.00.

Plate 3157. Pair of bolted urns, 15" tall, mark #242, $1,500.00 – 1,900.00 each.

Plate 3158. Vase, 5½" tall, mark #243, $550.00 – 700.00. Vase, 8½" tall, mark #244, $650.00 – 800.00.

Plate 3159. Vase, 9" tall, mark removed, $900.00 – 1,100.00.

Plate 3160. Vase, 11½" tall, mark #242, $1,100.00 – 1,300.00.

Plate 3161. Vase, 8¼" tall, mark #242, $900.00 – 1,100.00. Vase, 6¾" tall, mark #242, $800.00 – 950.00.

Plate 3162. Vase, 7" tall, mark #245, $800.00 – 950.00.

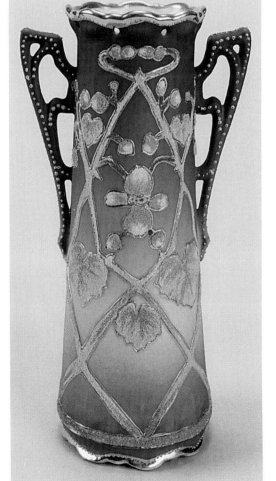

Plate 3164. Vase, 5½" tall, mark #242, $500.00 – 650.00. Vase, 4¼" tall, unmarked, $500.00 – 650.00.

Plate 3163. Vase, 9" tall, mark #242, $800.00 – 950.00.

Plate 3165. Vase, 5" tall, mark #242, $525.00 – 675.00.

Plate 3166. Vase, 9" tall, mark #242, $1,000.00 – 1,200.00.

Plate 3167. Vase, 15¼" tall, mark #242, $1,400.00 – 1,600.00.

Plate 3168. Vase, 8¼" tall, mark #245, $900.00 – 1,100.00.

Plate 3169. Vase, 7" tall, mark #245, $850.00 – 1,050.00.

Plate 3170. Vase, 13½" tall, mark #242, $1,200.00 – 1,400.00.

Plate 3171. Vase, 4¾" tall, mark #243, $475.00 – 575.00. Bowl, 6" wide, mark #242, $550.00 – 650.00. Vase, 4" tall, mark #242, $475.00 – 575.00.

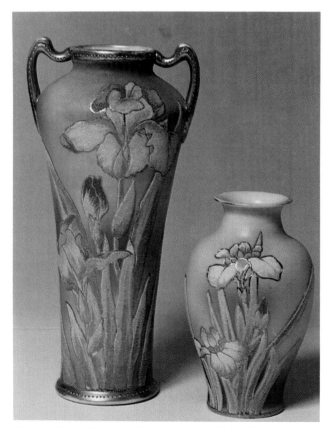

Plate 3172. Vase, 12" tall, mark #242, $1,100.00 – 1,300.00. Vase, 7¼" tall, mark #246, $600.00 – 700.00.

Plate 3173. Vase, 9½" tall, mark #244, $600.00 – 700.00.

Plate 3174. Vase, 8" tall, mark #245, $850.00 – 950.00.

Plate 3175. Vase, 10¾" tall, mark #244, $850.00 – 1,000.00.

Plate 3176. Vase, 12¼" tall, mark #242, $1,100.00 – 1,300.00.

Plate 3177. Vase, 4½" tall, mark #245, $475.00 – 575.00. Vase, 6" tall, mark #242, $525.00 – 600.00.

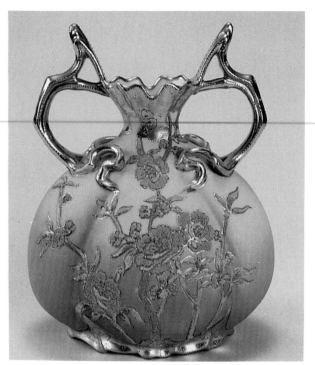

Plate 3178. Vase, 9" tall, mark #245, $900.00 – 1,000.00.

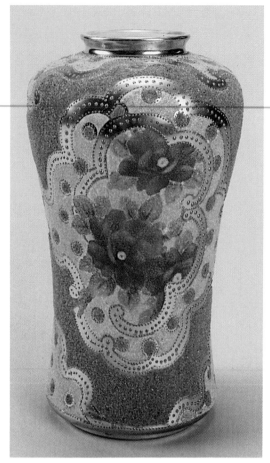

Plate 3179. Vase, 8½" tall, mark #245, $850.00 – 950.00.

Plate 3180. Vase, 11¼" tall, mark #242, $850.00 – 950.00.

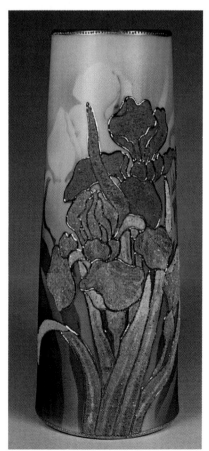

Plate 3181. Vase, 10" tall, mark #242, $1,500.00 — 1,800.00.

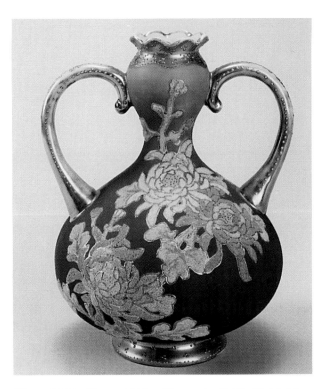

Plate 3182. Vase, 8¼" tall, mark #242, $850.00 – 950.00.

Plate 3183. Vase, 8¼" tall, mark #242, $850.00 – 950.00.

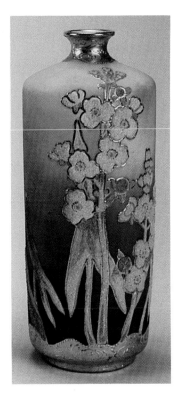

Plate 3184. Vase, 9" tall, mark #243, $800.00 – 900.00.

Plate 3185. Vase, 9¾" tall, mark #242, $850.00 – 950.00. Vase, 9¾" tall, mark #245, $850.00 – 950.00.

Plate 3186. Vase, 4" tall, mark #245, $550.00 – 650.00.

Plate 3187. Vase, 10" tall, mark #244, $850.00 – 950.00.
Vase, 13" tall, mark #242, $800.00 – 900.00.

Plate 3188. Vase, 6½" tall, mark #245, $650.00 – 750.00. Ewer, 5½" tall, mark #245, $500.00 – 600.00.

Plate 3189. Vase, 6¾" tall, mark #242, $550.00 – 650.00.

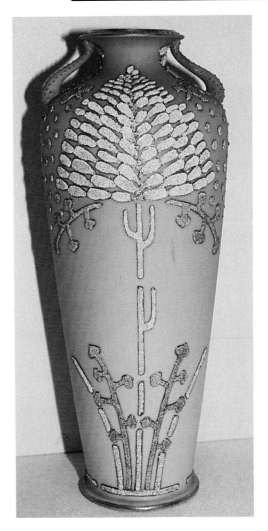

Plate 3190. Vase, 13½" tall, mark #242, $950.00 – 1,100.00.

Plate 3191. Vase, 4" tall, mark #242, $500.00 – 600.00. Vase, 7¼" tall, mark #242, $650.00 – 750.00.

Plate 3193. Vase, 4½" tall, mark #243, $600.00 – 700.00.

Plate 3192. Vase, 8¼" tall, mark #242, $750.00 – 850.00.

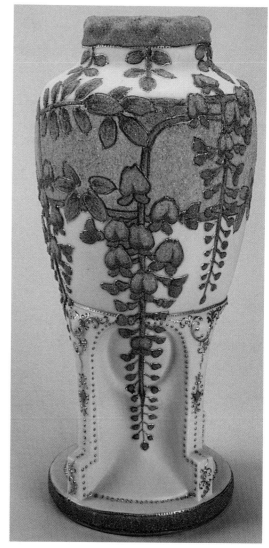

Plate 3194. Vase, 8½" tall, mark #244, $950.00 – 1,050.00.

Plate 3195. Vase, 12" tall, mark #242, $950.00 – 1,100.00.

Plate 3197. Vase, 8½" tall, mark #242, $750.00 – 850.00.
Vase, 7" tall, mark #242, $750.00 – 850.00.

Plate 3196. Vase, 6¼" tall, mark #242,
$600.00 – 700.00.

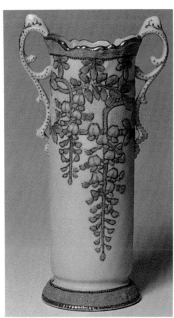

Plate 3198. Vase, 4½" tall, mark #242, $350.00 - 425.00. Vase, 5¼" tall, mark #242,
$350.00 - 425.00.

Plate 3199. Vase, 11¼" tall,
mark #242, $800.00 – 900.00.

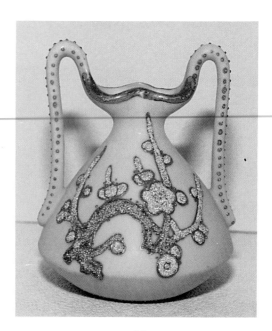

Plate 3201. Vase, 4¼" tall, mark #242, $325.00 – 400.00.

Plate 3200. Vase, 6½" tall, mark #242, $400.00 – 500.00. Vase, 9" tall, mark #242, $800.00 – 900.00.

Plate 3202. Vase, 6¾" tall, plate #242, $600.00 – 700.00.

Plate 3203. Vase, 6¾" tall, mark #242, $600.00 – 700.00.

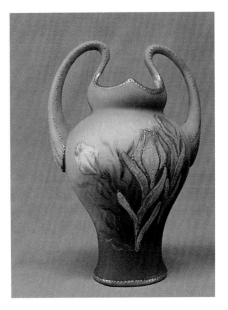

Plate 3205. Vase, 6¾" tall, mark #244, $625.00 – 725.00.

Plate 3204. Vase, 8¾" tall, mark #245, $650.00 – 750.00.

Plate 3206. Vase, 8¾" tall, mark #242, $725.00 – 825.00.
Vase, 7¼" tall, mark #245, $700.00 – 800.00.

Plate 3207. Vase, 8¾" tall, mark #244, $700.00 – 800.00.
Pitcher, 4¼" tall, mark #242, $425.00 – 500.00.

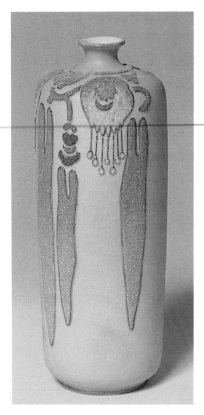

Plate 3209. Vase, 9" tall, mark #243, $900.00 – 1,000.00.
Vase, 9" tall, mark #243, $900.00 – 1,000.00.

Plate 3208. Vase, 8¾" tall, mark #244, $675.00 – 775.00.

Plate 3210. Vase, 9½" tall, mark #242, $900.00 – 1,000.00.

Plate 3211. Vase, 10½" tall, mark #244, $1,050.00 – 1,200.00.

Plate 3212. Vase, 6" tall, mark #244, $550.00 – 650.00.

Plate 3213. Ewer, 4" tall, mark #242, $350.00 – 425.00.

Plate 3214. Vase, 10¾" tall, mark #242, $925.00 – 1,025.00.

Plate 3215. Vase, 13¼" tall, mark #242, $1,100.00 – 1,250.00.

Plate 3216. Vase, 4½" tall, mark #242, $425.00 – 500.00. Pitcher, 4¼" tall, mark #242, $425.00 – 500.00.

Plate 3217. Vase, 6½" tall, mark #244, $750.00 – 850.00.

Plate 3218. Vase, 13½" tall, mark #242, $1,100.00 – 1,300.00.

Plate 3219. Vase, 6½" tall, mark #245, $700.00 – 800.00. Vase, 12½" tall, mark #242, $1,000.00 – 1,150.00.

Plate 3221. Vase, 11" tall, mark # 2 4 4 , $1,000.00 – 1,150.00.

Plate 3220. Vase, 9½" tall, mark #242, $800.00 – 900.00.

Plate 3222. Vase, 6" tall, mark #242, $550.00 – 650.00. Vase, 6¾" tall, mark #242, $550.00 – 650.00.

Plate 3223. Vase, 4¾" tall, mark #245, $450.00 – 550.00.

Plate 3224. Vase, 4¾" tall, mark #242, $450.00 – 550.00.

Plate 3225. Vase, 4¾" tall, mark #242, $450.00 – 550.00.

Plate 3226. Covered box (probably for a comb), 7" long, mark #242, $600.00 – 700.00.

Plate 3227. Dresser box, 3" tall, mark #242, $600.00 – 700.00.

Plate 3228. Vase, 4¼" tall, mark #242, $375.00 – 450.00.

Plate 3229. Vase, 10¼" tall, mark #242, $400.00 – 500.00. Vase, 5" tall, mark #242, $400.00 – 500.00.

Plate 3230. Vase, 9½" tall, mark #242, $1,000.00 – 1,200.00. Vase, 4" tall, mark #242, $600.00 – 700.00. Vase, 8½" tall, mark #242, $900.00 – 1,050.

Plate 3231. Vase, 4¼" tall, mark #242, $325.00 – 400.00.

Plate 3232. Vase, 5½" tall, mark #242, $500.00 – 600.00.

Plate 3233. Ferner, 8" tall, mark #243, $750.00 – 900.00.

Plate 3234. Ewer, 10" tall, mark #245, $900.00 – 1,000.00.

Plate 3236. Bowl, 4" tall, mark #242, $700.00 – 800.00.

Plate 3235. Vase, 7½" tall, mark #244, $800.00 – 950.00.

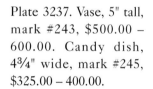

Plate 3237. Vase, 5" tall, mark #243, $500.00 – 600.00. Candy dish, 4¾" wide, mark #245, $325.00 – 400.00.

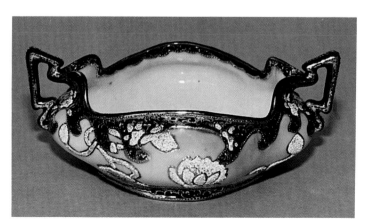

Plate 3238. Bowl, 7¼" wide, mark #242, $700.00 – 800.00.

Plate 3239. Coralene candy dish, 4¾" wide, mark #242, $325.00 – 400.00. Coralene candy dish, 4¾" wide, mark #242, $325.00 – 400.00.

EGYPTIAN DECOR

Plate 3240. Ferner, 7" tall, green mark #47, $600.00 – 700.00.

Plate 3241. Humidor, 5½" tall, green mark #47, $600.00 – 700.00.

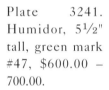

Plate 3242. Bowl, 10" wide including handles, green mark #47, $250.00 – 325.00.

Plate 3243. Inkwell, green mark #47, $400.00 – 500.00.

AMERICAN
INDIAN DECOR

Plate 3244. Ashtray with matchbox holder (relief molded), 3½" tall, green mark #47, $500.00 – 600.00. Ashtray, 5½" wide, green mark #47, $300.00 – 400.00. Ashtray with matchbox holder (relief molded), 3½" tall, green mark #47, $500.00 – 600.00.

Plate 3245. Pair of vases, blue mark #38, $350.00 – 425.00.

Plate 3246. Vase, 7" tall, blue mark #38, $300.00 – 400.00.

Plate 3247. Hanging plaque, 10" wide, green mark #47, $450.00 – 550.00.

Plate 3248. Bowl, 7½" wide, green mark #47, $225.00 – 275.00.

Plate 3249. Stein, 7" tall, green mark #47, $700.00 – 800.00.

Plate 3250. Relish dish, 8½" long, blue mark #52, $175.00 – 225.00.

Plate 3251. Candlestick, 8" tall, green mark #47, $325.00 – 375.00.

MAN ON CAMEL
SCENE

Plate 3252. Vase, 13" tall, green mark #47, $725.00 – 825.00.

Plate 3253. Vase, 11" tall, green mark #47, $525.00 – 600.00.

Plate 3254. Pair of mirror image vases, 6" tall, mark #229, $350.00 – 400.00 each.

225

Plate 3255. Vase, 7½" tall, green mark #47, $400.00 – 500.00. Mug, 5½" tall, green mark #47, $350.00 – 400.00.

Plate 3257. Vase, 7¾" tall, green mark #47, $400.00 – 500.00.

Plate 3256. Vase, 7¾" tall, green mark #47, $325.00 – 400.00.

Plate 3258. Candlestick, 8" tall, green mark #47, $325.00 – 375.00.

Plate 3259. Hanging plaque, 10" wide, green mark #47, $500.00 – 600.00.

Plate 3261. Ashtray and matchbox holder, 3½" tall, green mark #47, $275.00 – 350.00.

Plate 3260. Hanging plaque, 10" wide, green mark #47, $350.00 – 425.00.

Plate 3262. Vase, 11¼" tall, magenta mark #110, $425.00 – 500.00.

Plate 3263. Pair of candlesticks, 8" tall, green mark #47, $800.00 – 900.00 pr.

WOODLAND PATTERN

Plate 3264. Vase, 6¼" tall, mark #229, $350.00 – 400.00.

Plate 3265. Vase, 7" tall, green mark #47, $600.00 – 700.00. Vase, 7¾" tall, blue mark #52, $400.00 – 500.00.

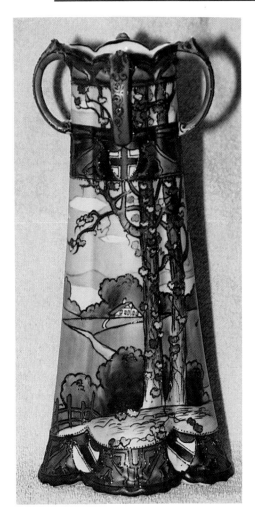

Plate 3267. Vase, 10" tall, blue mark #52, $800.00 – 1,000.00.

Plate 3266. Vase, 13" tall, green mark #50, $500.00 – 600.00.

Plate 3268. Vase, 7¼" tall, green mark #47, $750.00 – 850.00.

Plate 3269. Vase, 8" tall, blue mark #52, $775.00 – 900.00.

Plate 3270. Powder box, 5" wide, green mark #47, $175.00 – 225.00. Powder box, 5½" wide, green mark #47, $175.00 – 225.00.

Plate 3271. Vase, 7" tall, green mark #52, $375.00 – 500.00.

Plate 3272. Ewer, 13" tall, blue mark #52, $675.00 – 850.00.

Plate 3273. Bowl, 7" wide, green mark #47, $175.00 – 225.00.

Plate 3274. Hanging plaque, 11" diameter, blue mark #52, $750.00 – 900.00.

Plate 3275. Dish, 8" long, green mark #47, $150.00 – 200.00.

Plate 3276. Bowl, 7¼" wide, blue mark #47, $175.00 – 225.00.

Plate 3277. Dish, 7¼" long, green mark #47, $150.00 – 200.00.

Plate 3278. Matchbox holder with ashtray, 3½" tall, blue mark #52, $400.00 – 500.00.

Plate 3279. Tea set, comes with six cups and saucers, green mark #47, $1,100.00 – 1,300.00.

Plate 3281. Salt and pepper shakers, green mark #47, $125.00 – 165.00.

Plate 3280. Dresser set, blue mark #52, $900.00 – 1,100.00.

Plate 3282. Bowl, 6" wide, green mark #47, $150.00 – 200.00. Bowl, 5¾" wide, green mark #52, $150.00 – 200.00.

Plate 3283. Salt and pepper shakers, 3¾" tall, green mark #47, $125.00 – 165.00. Mustard jar, 3½" tall, green mark #47, $175.00 – 225.00.

Plate 3284. Bowl, 8" wide, blue mark #52, $200.00 – 250.00. Bowl, 7½" wide, mark #4, $175.00 – 225.00.

Plate 3285. Bowl, 8" long, blue mark #52, $175.00 – 225.00.

Plate 3286. Bowl, 5" wide, blue mark #52, $175.00 – 225.00.

Plate 3287. Ladle, unmarked, $150.00 – 200.00.

Plate 3288. Nappy, 7½" wide, green mark #47, $200.00 – 250.00.

Plate 3290. Chamberstick, blue mark #47, $350.00 – 425.00.

Plate 3289. Bowl, 8½" wide, blue mark #52, $225.00 – 275.00.

Plate 3291. Covered box, 5" long, blue mark #47, $275.00 – 325.00. Matchbox holder and ashtray, 2½" tall, green mark #47, $200.00 – 250.00.

GALLE PATTERN

Plate 3292. Bowl, 6" wide, blue mark #52, $175.00 – 250.00. Bowl, 6½" wide, green mark #47, $185.00 – 260.00.

Plate 3293. Vase, 8" tall, blue mark #52, $350.00 – 425.00.

Plate 3295. Vase, 8½" tall, blue mark #52, $350.00 – 425.00.

Plate 3296. Hanging plaque, 10" wide, blue mark #52, $350.00 – 425.00.

Plate 3294. Vase, 11" tall, blue mark #47, $425.00 – 525.00.

BOLTED URNS

Plate 3297. Bolted urn, 17½" tall, green mark #47, $2,000.00 – 2,400.00.

Plate 3298. Bolted urn, 18" tall, green mark #47, $1,100.00 – 1,300.00.

Plate 3299. Bolted urn, 17" tall, blue mark #47, $2,000.00 – 2,400.00.

Plate 3300. Bolted urn, 13¾" tall, green mark #47, $1,000.00 – 1,200.00.

Plate 3301. Bolted urn, 16" tall, blue mark #47, $1,300.00 – 1,500.00.

Plate 3302. Bolted urn, 16" tall, green mark #47, $1,300.00 – 1,500.00.

Plate 3303. Bolted urn, 16½" tall, green mark #47, $1,900.00 – 2,300.00.

Plate 3304. Bolted urn, 9½" tall, green mark #47, $425.00 – 525.00.

Plate 3307. Bolted urn, 12" tall, mark #47, $800.00 – 950.00.

Plate 3306. Bolted urn, 15¼" tall, green mark #47, $1,400.00 – 1,600.00.

Plate 3305. Bolted urn, 14¾" tall, blue mark #52, 950.00 – 1,100.00.

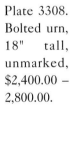

Plate 3308. Bolted urn, 18" tall, unmarked, $2,400.00 – 2,800.00.

Plate 3309. Bolted urn, 13¾" tall, unmarked, $900.00 – 1,100.00.

Plate 3310. Bolted urn, 16" tall, green mark #47, $1,300.00 – 1,500.00.

Plate 3313. Covered urn, 8½" tall, blue mark #52, $800.00 – 900.00.

Plate 3312. Bolted urn, 12" tall, green mark #47, $750.00 – 850.00.

Plate 3311. Bolted urn, 15½" tall, blue mark #52, $900.00 – 1,100.00.

Plate 3314. Covered urn, 8¾" tall, mark #101, $500.00 – 600.00.

Plate 3316. Bolted urn, 19½" tall, blue mark #52, $1,900.00 – 2,200.00.

Plate 3315. Bolted urn, 18" tall, green mark #47, $1,600.00 – 1,800.00.

Plate 3317. Covered bolted urn, 15½" tall, blue mark #52, $1,900.00 – 2,200.00.

Plate 3318. Bolted urn, 12" tall, green mark #47, $700.00 – 800.00.

Plate 3319. Bolted covered urn, 13½" tall, mark #89, $1,300.00 – 1,500.00.

Plate 3320. Bolted urn, 12" tall, green mark #47, $700.00 – 800.00.

VASES

Plate 3321. Vase, 6" tall, green mark #47, $225.00 – 275.00. Vase, 8" tall, green mark #47, $300.00 – 375.00. Vase, 8" tall, green mark #47, $300.00 – 375.00.

Plate 3322. Vase, 11" tall, green mark #47, $350.00 – 425.00.

Plate 3323. Vase, 11" tall, blue mark #52, $350.00 – 425.00.

Plate 3324. Vase, 7" tall, green mark #52, $300.00 – 375.00.

Plate 3325. Vase, 8¾" tall, mark #47, $300.00 – 375.00.

Plate 3326. Vase, 12¼" tall, green mark #52, $650.00 – 800.00.

Plate 3327. Vase, 12¼" tall, green mark #52, $650.00 – 800.00.

Plate 3328. Vase, 8½" tall, blue mark #52, $500.00 – 600.00.

Plate 3329. Vase, 12½" tall, green mark #47, $350.00 – 425.00.

Plate 3330. Vase, 14" tall, green mark #47, $650.00 – 800.00.

Plate 3331. Pair of vases, 11½" tall, green mark #47, $325.00 – 400.00 each.

Plate 3332. Vase, 11¼" tall, green mark #52, $425.00 – 500.00.

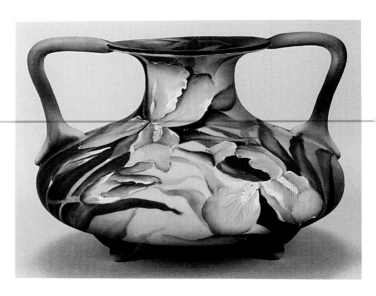

Plate 3334. Vase, 4¾" tall, mark #89, $425.00 – 475.00.

Plate 3333. Vase, 12" tall, unmarked, $350.00 – 425.00.

Plate 3337. Vase, 10¾" tall, blue mark #52, $350.00 – 425.00.

Plate 3335. Vase, 6½" tall, green mark #47, $275.00 – 325.00.

Plate 3336. Vase, 11" tall, blue mark #52, $325.00 – 400.00.

Plate 3338. Vase, 9½" tall, mark #47, $300.00 – 375.00.

Plate 3339. Vase, 8" tall, green mark #47, $275.00 – 350.00.

Plate 3340. Vase, 11" tall, blue mark #52, $375.00 – 475.00.

Plate 3341. Vase, 7½" tall, $275.00 – 350.00.

Plate 3342. Vase, 7¼" tall, blue mark #47, $275.00 – 350.00.

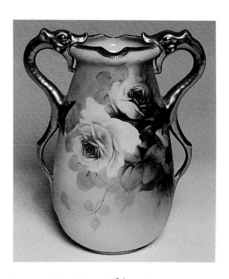

Plate 3343. Vase, 7¾" tall, blue mark #47, $325.00 – 400.00.

Plate 3345. Vase, 10" tall, green mark #47, $325.00 – 400.00. Vase, 12" tall, blue mark #52, $375.00 – 450.00.

Plate 3344. Vase, 9" tall, mark #47, $325.00 – 400.00

Plate 3346. Vase, 10¼" tall, blue mark #52, $325.00 – 400.00.

Plate 3347. Vase, 12" tall, green mark #47, $400.00 – 500.00.

Plate 3348. Pair of vases, 11½" tall, blue mark #52, $425.00 – 525.00 each.

Plate 3350. Vase, 7½" tall, green mark #47, $225.00 – 300.00.

Plate 3349. Vase, 7" tall, green mark #15, $200.00 – 275.00.

Plate 3351. Pair of vases, 9½" tall, green mark #47, $225.00 – 300.00 each.

Plate 3352. Vase, 9¾" tall, unmarked, $350.00 – 425.00.

Plate 3354. Pair of vases, 7" tall, green mark #52, $275.00 – 325.00 each.

Plate 3353. Vase, 12¾" tall, mark #47, $400.00 – 500.00.

Plate 3355. Pair of vases, 8½" tall, blue mark #52, $300.00 – 400.00 each.

Plate 3356. Vase, 10" tall, green mark #47, $325.00 – 400.00.

Plate 3357. Vase, 11½" tall, green mark #47, $400.00 – 500.00.

Plate 3360. Vase, 10" tall, green mark #47, $275.00 – 350.00.

Plate 3359. Vase, 9" tall, green mark #47, $275.00 – 350.00.

Plate 3358. Vase, 9" tall, blue mark #52, $275.00 – 350.00.

Plate 3363. Vase, 10" tall, blue mark #38, $350.00 – 425.00.

Plate 3361. Vase, 6" tall, blue mark #52, $125.00 – 160.00.

Plate 3362. Vase, 13" tall, unmarked, $525.00 – 625.00.

Plate 3364. Vase, 10" tall, green mark #47, $325.00 – 400.00.

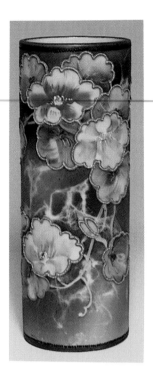

Plate 3365. Vase, 7½" tall, green mark #47, $275.00 – 325.00.

Plate 3366. Vase, 10" tall, green mark #47, $325.00 – 400.00.

Plate 3367. Vase, 9" tall, green mark #47, $250.00 – 300.00.

Plate 3368. Vase, 12" tall, green mark #52, $400.00 – 500.00.

Plate 3369. Vase, 11½" tall, mark #52, $400.00 – 500.00.

Plate 3370. Vase, 10" tall, blue mark #52, $350.00 – 425.00.

Plate 3371. Vase, 18½" tall, blue mark #47, $1,400.00 – 1,700.00.

Plate 3372. Pair of vases, 8" tall, blue mark #47, $325.00 – 400.00 each.

Plate 3373. Vase, 11" tall, green mark #47, $300.00 – 375.00.

Plate 3374. Vase, 10½" tall, blue mark #38, $275.00 – 350.00.

Plate 3375. Vase, 3" tall, blue mark #52, $165.00 – 225.00.

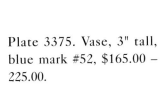

Plate 3376. Vase, 17¾" tall, unmarked, $1,200.00 – 1,400.00.

Plate 3378. Vase, 6½" tall, green mark #52, $275.00 – 325.00.

Plate 3379. Vase, 10" tall, green mark #47, $300.00 – 375.00.

Plate 3377. Vase, 24¼" tall, blue mark #52, $3,000.00 – 3,500.00.

Plate 3382. Vase, 5¼" tall, mark #89, $125.00 – 160.00.

Plate 3381. Vase, 10" tall, blue mark #52, $350.00 – 425.00.

Plate 3380. Vase, 8½" tall, blue mark #52, $275.00 – 350.00.

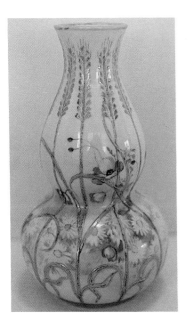

Plate 3383. Vase, 9½" tall, green mark #47, $275.00 – 325.00.

Plate 3384. Vase, 10" tall, green mark #47, $325.00 – 400.00.

Plate 3385. Vase, 7" tall, green mark #47, $250.00 – 325.00.

Plate 3387. Vase, 11½" tall, blue mark #38, $250.00 – 325.00.

Plate 3386. Vase, 9½" tall, mark #17, $225.00 – 275.00.

Plate 3388. Vase, 11½" tall, mark #47, $350.00 – 425.00.

Plate 3391. Vase, 8" tall, green mark #52, $300.00 – 375.00.

Plate 3390. Vase, 12½" tall, mark #47, $325.00 – 400.00.

Plate 3389. Vase, 7¼" tall, green mark #47, $150.00 – 200.00.

Plate 3392. Vase, 12" tall, mark #52, $400.00 – 500.00.

Plate 3393. Vase, 11½" tall, blue mark #52, $400.00 – 500.00.

Plate 3394. Vase, 6¾" tall, mark #6, $225.00 – 275.00.

Plate 3396. Vase, 7" tall, green mark #47, $150.00 – 200.00.

Plate 3395. Vase, 10½" tall, green mark #47, $350.00 – 425.00. Vase, 6½" tall, green mark #47, $275.00 – 350.00.

Plate 3397. Vase, 10" tall, blue mark #52, $350.00 – 425.00.

Plate 3400. Vase, 8½" tall, blue mark #52, $450.00 – 550.00.

Plate 3399. Vase, 11½" tall, green mark #47, $300.00 – 375.00.

Plate 3398. Vase, 11½" tall, blue mark #52, $325.00 – 400.00.

Plate 3402. Vase, 10" tall, green mark #47, $375.00 – 450.00.

Plate 3401. Vase, 12¼" tall, blue mark #52, $425.00 – 500.00.

Plate 3403. Vase, 8½" tall, green mark #47 $450.00 – 525.00.

Plate 3404. Vase, 11½" tall, green mark #47, $325.00 – 400.00.

Plate 3405. Vase, 9½" tall, green mark #47, $300.00 – 375.00.

Plate 3406. Vase, 10¼" tall, blue mark #38, $250.00 – 300.00.

Plate 3407. Vase, 5¼" tall, green mark #47, $150.00 – 200.00.

Plate 3408. Vase, 14" tall, green mark #47, $400.00 – 500.00.

Plate 3409. Vase, 15½" tall, blue mark #52, $1,300.00 – 1,500.00.

Plate 3410. Vase, 12" tall, mark #91, $175.00 – 250.00.

Plate 3411. Vase, 8" tall, blue mark #52, $325.00 – 400.00.

Plate 3412. Vase, 12½" tall, green mark #4, $375.00 – 450.00.

Plate 3413. Vase, 10½" tall, blue mark #71, $300.00 – 375.00.

Plate 3414. Vase, 5½" tall, green mark #47, $100.00 – 150.00.

Plate 3415. Vase, 11½" tall, green mark #47, $250.00 – 325.00.

Plate 3416. Vase, 9½" tall, blue mark #47, $325.00 – 400.00.

Plate 3417. Vase, 9" tall, blue mark #47, $300.00 – 375.00.

Plate 3418. Vase, 12" tall, blue mark #38, $250.00 – 300.00.

Plate 3419. Vase, 15¼" tall, vase, blue mark #96, $400.00 – 500.00.

Plate 3420. Vase, 15¼" tall, green mark #47, $2,000.00 – 2,500.00.

Plate 3421. Vase, 15¾" tall, green mark #47, $2,000.00 – 2,500.00.

Plate 3422. Vase, 18" tall, blue mark #52, $1,500.00 – 1,800.00.

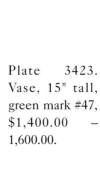

Plate 3423. Vase, 15" tall, green mark #47, $1,400.00 – 1,600.00.

Plate 3424. (front row) Vase, 4½" tall, green mark #47, $135.00 – 175.00. Vase, 5" tall, green mark #52, $100.00 – 140.00. Vase, 4½" tall, green mark #52, $90.00 – 135.00. (back row) Vase, 5½" tall, green mark #47, $135.00 – 175.00. Vase, 4" tall, green mark #47, $85.00 – 125.00. Vase, 5" tall, blue mark #52, $125.00 – 175.00. Vase, 6¼" tall, blue mark #52, $200.00 – 250.00.

Plate 3425. Vase, 11" tall, green mark #47, $325.00 – 400.00.

Plate 3427. Vase, 10¾" tall, green mark #47, $325.00 – 400.00. Pair of candlesticks, green mark #47, $550.00 – 700.00 pair.

Plate 3426. Vase, 10½" tall, green mark #47, $325.00 – 400.00.

Plate 3429. Vase, 12¾"
tall, green mark #47,
$125.00 – 160.00.

Plate 3428. Vase, 12½" tall, blue mark #52,
$325.00 – 400.00.

Plate 3430. Vase, 5½" tall, green mark #47, $125.00 – 160.00. Vase, 6"
tall, green mark #47, $125.00 – 160.00. Vase, 5½" tall, green mark #47,
$125.00 – 160.00.

Plate 3431. Vase, 14" tall, mark
#47, $700.00 – 850.00.

Plate 3433. Vase, 7¾" tall, mark #47, $250.00 – 300.00.

Plate 3434. Vase, 9½" tall, blue mark #52, $300.00 – 375.00.

Plate 3432. Vase, 6½" tall, blue mark #52, $275.00 – 350.00.

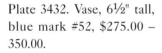

Plate 3435. Vase, 12" tall, mark #91 (artist signed), $275.00 – 325.00.

Plate 3436. Basket vase, 10" tall, green mark #47, $500.00 – 600.00.

Plate 3437. Pair of vases, 8½" tall, (front and back views), $250.00 – 300.00 each.

Plate 3438. Vase, 12" tall, blue mark #38, $300.00 – 375.00.

Plate 3439. Vase, 12¼" tall, green mark #47, $550.00 – 650.00.

Plate 3440. Pair of vases, 7½" tall, blue mark #38, $200.00 – 250.00 each.

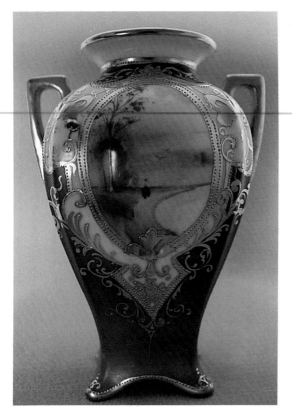

Plate 3441. Vase, 7¼" tall, green mark #47, $250.00 – 300.00.

Plate 3443. Vase, 14" tall, blue mark #52, $750.00 – 850.00.

Plate 3442. Vase, 13" tall, green mark #47, $300.00 – 375.00.

Plate 3444. Vase, 8" tall, green mark #47, $325.00 – 400.00.

Plate 3445. Vase, 10" tall, green mark #47, $400.00 – 500.00.

Plate 3446. Vase, 4" tall, green mark #47, $225.00 – 275.00.

Plate 3447. Vase, 7½" tall, green mark #47, $225.00 – 275.00.

Plate 3448. Vase, 9½" tall, green mark #47, $350.00 – 425.00.

Plate 3449. Vase, 10" tall, green mark #47, $400.00 – 475.00.

Plate 3450. Vase, 9" tall, green mark #47, $350.00 – 425.00.

Plate 3451. Vase, 9" tall, green mark #47, $350.00 – 425.00.

Plate 3452. Vase, 8½" tall, green mark #47, $350.00 – 425.00.

Plate 3453. Vase, 9½" tall, green mark #47, $300.00 – 350.00.

Plate 3454. Vase, 6¼" tall, green mark #47, $250.00 – 300.00.

Plate 3455. Ewer, 11½" tall, blue mark #52, $375.00 – 475.00.

Plate 3456. Vase, 9¾" tall, green mark #47, $300.00 – 350.00.

Plate 3457. Vase, 10" tall, blue mark #52, $400.00 – 500.00.

Plate 3458. Vase, 5½" tall, mark #52, $275.00 – 335.00.

Plate 3459. Vase, 8" tall, blue mark #47, $275.00 – 335.00.

Plate 3460. Vase, 13½" tall, green mark #47, $750.00 – 900.00.

Plate 3461. Vase, 8" tall, green mark #47, $375.00 – 450.00. Vase, 8" tall, green mark #47, $375.00 – 450.00.

Plate 3462. Vase, 6½" tall, green mark #47, $300.00 – 350.00.

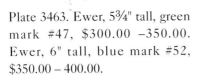

Plate 3463. Ewer, 5¾" tall, green mark #47, $300.00 –350.00. Ewer, 6" tall, blue mark #52, $350.00 – 400.00.

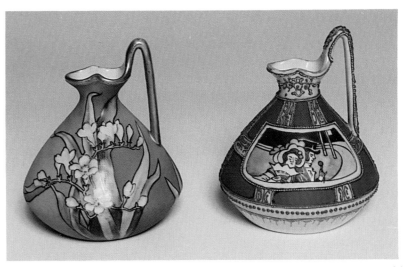

Plate 3464. Pair of mirror image vases, 9" tall, mark #229, $550.00 – 625.00 each.

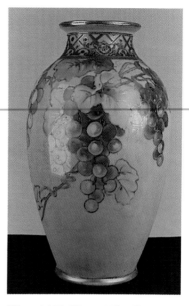

Plate 3465. Vase, 13" tall, green mark #47, $400.00 – 500.00.

Plate 3466. Vase, 7¼" tall, green mark #47, $175.00 – 235.00.

Plate 3467. Vase, 10" tall, green mark #47, $350.00 – 400.00. Vase, 9" tall, green mark #47, $350.00 – 400.00.

Plate 3468. Vase, 8¾" tall, green mark #47, $275.00 – 325.00.

Plate 3469. Vase, 8" tall, green mark #47, $300.00 – 475.00.

Plate 3470. Ewer, 7¼" tall, mark #4, $250.00 – 300.00.

HANGING PLAQUES

Plate 3471. Hanging plaque, 10" wide, green mark #47, $300.00 – 350.00.

Plate 3472. Hanging plaque, 11" wide, blue mark #52, $300.00 – 350.00.

Plate 3473. Hanging plaque, 10" wide, green mark #47, $300.00 – 350.00.

Plate 3474. Hanging plaque, 11" wide, blue mark #47, $325.00 – 375.00.

Plate 3475. Hanging plaque, 10¼" wide, green mark #47, $300.00 – 350.00.

Plate 3476. Hanging plaque, 10½" wide, green mark #47, $300.00 – 375.00.

Plate 3477. Hanging plaque, 10" wide, green mark #47, $300.00 – 350.00.

Plate 3478. Hanging plaque, 10" wide, blue mark #52, $300.00 – 350.00.

Plate 3479. Hanging plaque, 11" wide, green mark #47, $275.00 – 325.00.

Plate 3480. Hanging plaque, 10" wide, blue mark #52, $300.00 – 350.00.

Plate 3481. Hanging plaque, 9" wide, green mark #47, $275.00 – 325.00.

Plate 3482. Hanging plaque, 9½" wide, green mark #52, $275.00 – 325.00.

Plate 3483. Hanging plaque, 10¾" wide, blue mark #52, $425.00 – 475.00.

Plate 3484. Hanging plaque, 9" wide, green mark #47, $300.00 – 350.00.

Plate 3485. Hanging plaque, 10" wide, green mark #47, $300.00 – 350.00.

Plate 3486. Hanging plaque, 11" wide, blue mark #52, $450.00 – 550.00.

Plate 3487. Hanging plaque, 8½" wide, blue mark #52, $275.00 – 325.00.

Plate 3488. Hanging plaque, 10" wide, green mark #47, $300.00 – 350.00.

Plate 3489. Hanging plaque, 10" wide, green mark #47, $300.00 – 350.00.

Plate 3490. Hanging plaque, 7¾" wide, blue mark #47, $225.00 – 275.00.

Plate 3491. Hanging plaque, 8¾" wide, green mark #47, $350.00 – 400.00.

Plate 3492. Hanging plaque, 9" wide, green mark #47, $300.00 – 350.00.

Plate 3493. Hanging plaque, 10" wide, green mark #47, $425.00 – 500.00.

Plate 3494. Hanging plaque, 7½" wide, green mark #47, $275.00 – 350.00.

Plate 3495. Hanging plaque, 9½" wide, green mark #47, $325.00 – 400.00.

Plate 3496. Hanging plaque, 10" wide, blue mark #52, $325.00 – 400.00.

Plate 3497. Hanging plaque, 10" wide, blue mark #47, $325.00 – 400.00.

Plate 3498. Hanging plaque, 8¾" wide, mark #17, $300.00 – 375.00.

Plate 3499. Hanging plaque, 8" wide, green mark #47, $275.00 – 325.00.

Plate 3500. Hanging plaque, 10" wide, green mark #47, $325.00 – 400.00.

Plate 3501. Hanging plaque, 9" wide, green mark #47, $325.00 – 400.00.

Plate 3502. Hanging plaque, 7¾" wide, green mark #47, $275.00 – 325.00.

Plate 3503. Hanging plaque, 10" wide, green mark #47, $325.00 – 400.00.

Plate 3504. Hanging plaque, 10¼" wide, green mark #47, $325.00 – 400.00.

Plate 3505. Hanging plaque, 9" wide, green mark #47, $300.00 – 375.00.

Plate 3506. Hanging plaque, 9" wide, green mark #47, $300.00 – 375.00.

Plate 3507. Hanging plaque, 10" wide, green mark #47, $325.00 – 400.00.

Plate 3508. Hanging plaque, 9" wide, green mark #47, $300.00 – 375.00.

Plate 3509. Hanging plaque, 9" wide, green mark #47, $300.00 – 375.00.

Plate 3510. Hanging plaque, 8¾" wide, green mark #47, $300.00 – 375.00.

Plate 3511. Hanging plaque, 8½" wide, mark #17, $250.00 – 300.00.

Plate 3512. Hanging plaque, 10" wide, green mark #47, $325.00 – 400.00.

Plate 3513. Hanging plaque, 8½" wide, blue mark #47, $300.00 – 375.00.

Plate 3514. Hanging plaque, 10" wide, green mark #47, $325.00 – 400.00.

Plate 3515. Hanging plaque, 7¾" wide, green mark #47, $250.00 – 300.00.

Plate 3516. Hanging plaque, 9" wide, blue mark #52, $300.00 – 375.00.

Plate 3517. Hanging plaque, 10½" wide, green mark #47, $325.00 – 400.00.

Plate 3518. Hanging plaque, 8½" wide, mark #17, $275.00 – 350.00.

Plate 3519. Hanging plaque, 11" wide, green mark #47, $325.00 – 400.00.

Plate 3520. Hanging plaque, 12" wide, green mark #47, $600.00 – 700.00.

Plate 3521. Hanging plaque, 10" wide, green mark #47, $325.00 – 400.00.

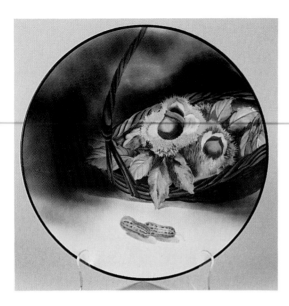

Plate 3522. Hanging plaque, 12¼" wide, green mark #47, $450.00 – 525.00.

Plate 3523. Hanging plaque, 7¾" wide, green mark #47, $225.00 – 275.00.

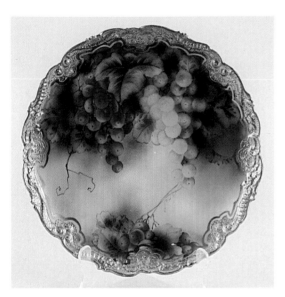

Plate 3524. Hanging plaque, 12½" wide, blue mark #52, $450.00 – 525.00.

Plate 3525. Hanging plaque, 10" wide, green mark #47, $325.00 – 400.00.

Plate 3526. Hanging plaque, 11" wide, green mark #47, $350.00 – 425.00.

Plate 3527. Smoke set, tray is 7¾" in diameter, matchbox is 2¾" tall, humidor is 5" tall, green mark #47, $600.00 – 700.00.

Plate 3528. Humidor, with match striker finial, 8" tall, green mark #47, $850.00 – 1,000.00.

Plate 3529. Humidor, 7" tall, green mark #47, $700.00 – 800.00.

SMOKE SETS & HUMIDORS

Plate 3530. Smoke set, tray is 9¾" wide, green mark #47, $650.00 – 750.00.

Plate 3531. Humidor, 9" tall, green mark #47, $525.00 – 600.00.

Plate 3532. Humidor, 7" tall, green mark #47, $625.00 – 725.00.

Plate 3533. Smoke set, tray is 7¾" in diameter, humidor is 5½" tall, green mark #47, $700.00 – 800.00.

Plate 3534. Humidor, 5" tall, green mark #47, $500.00 – 600.00.

Plate 3535. Humidor, 5½" tall, mark scratched off, $325.00 – 400.00.

Plate 3536. Humidor, 4¼" tall, green mark #47, $325.00 – 400.00. Humidor, 4½" tall, green mark #47, $350.00 – 425.00.

Plate 3537. Humidor, 7"
tall, green mark #47,
$700.00 – 825.00.

Plate 3538. Humidor, 7"
tall, green mark #47,
$500.00 – 600.00.

Plate 3539. Humidor, 6" tall, green
mark #47, $525.00 – 625.00.

Plate 3540. Smoke set, tray is 7½" in diameter, green
mark #47, $650.00 – 750.00.

Plate 3541. Humidor,
5½" tall, green mark #47,
$500.00 – 600.00.

Plate 3544. Humidor, 6¼" tall, green mark #47, $600.00 – 700.00.

Plate 3542. Humidor, 6½" tall, mark #17, $375.00 – 450.00.

Plate 3543. Humidor, 7" tall, green mark #47, $550.00 – 625.00.

Plate 3545. Humidor, 6½" tall, green mark #47, $550.00 – 650.00.

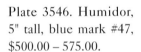

Plate 3546. Humidor, 5" tall, blue mark #47, $500.00 – 575.00.

Plate 3547. Humidor, 7½" tall, blue mark #38, $400.00 – 475.00.

Plate 3548. Humidor, 5½" tall, mark #27, $400.00 – 475.00.

Plate 3549. Smoke set, tray is 10" in diameter, green mark #47, $850.00 – 950.00.

Plate 3550. Humidor, 6" tall, green mark #47, $625.00 – 700.00.

Plate 3551. Ashtray, 4¾" long, green mark #47, $125.00 – 160.00.
Ashtray, 4¾" long, green mark #47, $100.00 – 150.00.

Plate 3552. Ashtray, 5½" wide, blue mark #67, $110.00 – 160.00.

Plate 3553. Ashtray, 6¾" wide, mark #38, $125.00 – 160.00.

Plate 3554. Humidor, 5½" tall, green mark #47, $500.00 – 600.00.

Plate 3555. Smoke set, green mark #47, $600.00 – 700.00.

Plate 3556. Ashtray, 4¾" wide, green mark #47, $175.00 – 225.00.

Plate 3557. Ashtray, green mark #47, $125.00 – 160.00.

Plate 3558. Ashtray, 5" wide, green mark #47, $175.00 – 225.00.

Plate 3559. Humidor, 6" tall, green mark #47, $575.00 – 675.00.

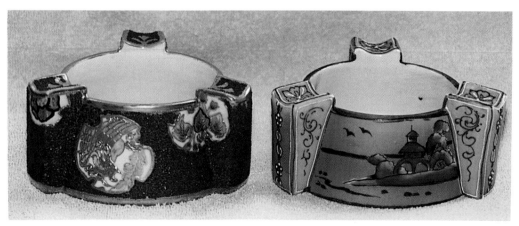

Plate 3560. Ashtray, 5½" wide, green mark #47, $175.00 – 235.00. Ashtray, 5¼" wide, green mark #47, $175.00 – 235.00.

Plate 3561. Ashtray, 6½" wide, blue mark #38, $185.00 – 250.00.

Plate 3562. Ashtray, 5" wide, green mark #47, $110.00 – 150.00.

Plate 3563. Ashtray, 5¼" tall, green mark #47, $175.00 – 235.00.

Plate 3564. Combination matchbox holder and ashtray, 3½" tall, green mark #47, $200.00 – 275.00.

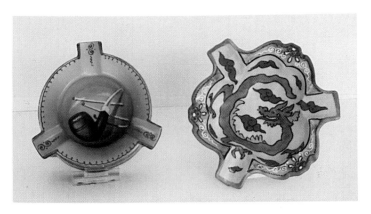

Plate 3565. Ashtray, green mark #47, $150.00 – 200.00. Ashtray, green mark #47, $135.00 – 175.00.

Plate 3566. Side view of 3564, $200.00 – 275.00.

Plate 3567. Smoke set, cigarette holder, 3" tall, match holder, 3" tall, tray is 5" long, green mark #47, $300.00 – 400.00.

Plate 3568. Cigar ashtray, 6" long, blue mark #52, $135.00 – 175.00.

Plate 3569. Ashtray, 5" wide, green mark #47, $200.00 – 250.00.

Plate 3570. Ashtray, 7¾" wide, green mark #47, $200.00 – 250.00.

Plate 3571. Cigar ashtray, 3" long, blue mark #52, $100.00 – 150.00.

Plate 3572. Cigar ashtray, 5" wide, green mark #47, $300.00 – 400.00.

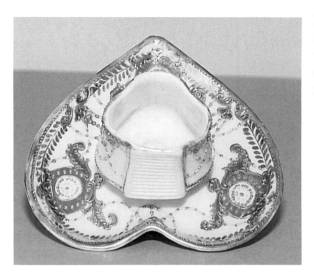

Plate 3573. Match holder/striker/ashtray, 2" tall, mark #52, $225.00 – 275.00.

Plate 3574. Combination match holder and ashtray, green mark #47, $200.00 – 275.00.

Plate 3575. Cigar holder and ashtray, 6½" long, green mark #47, $200.00 – 275.00.

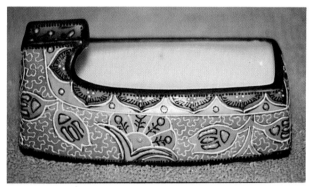

Plate 3576. Cigar holder and ashtray, 4" long, green mark #47, $200.00 – 275.00.

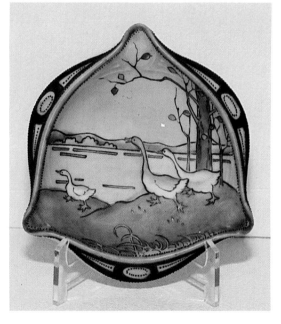

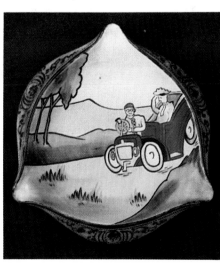

Plate 3577. Ashtray, 5½" wide, green mark #47, $250.00 – 300.00.

Plate 3578. Ashtray, 5½" wide, blue mark #47, $200.00 – 250.00.

Plate 3579. Hanging matchbox holder (molded strikers on sides), 4½" tall, blue mark #52, $225.00 – 275.00.

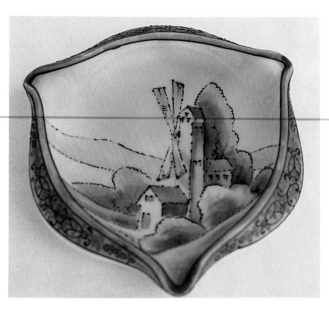

Plate 3580. Ashtray, 5½" wide, blue mark #52, $200.00 – 250.00.

Plate 3581. Hanging double matchbox holder, 3½" long, blue mark #52, $250.00 – 300.00.

Plate 3582. Hanging matchbox holder, green mark #47, $225.00 – 275.00.

Plate 3583. Ashtray, 5½" wide, green mark #47, $200.00 – 250.00.

Plate 3584. Match holder/ashtray, 3½" tall, blue mark #52, $200.00 – 250.00.

Plate 3585. Match holder, 2½" tall, green mark #47, $200.00 – 250.00.

Plate 3586. Pipe holder, 4" long, blue mark #84, $175.00 – 225.00.

Plate 3587. Ashtray, 5¼" wide, green mark #47, $200.00 – 275.00.

Plate 3588. Hanging double matchbox holder, 5" long, green mark #47, $225.00 – 275.00.

Plate 3589. Hanging match safe, bottom compartment is for used matches, 4" tall, blue mark #52, $275.00 – 350.00.

Plate 3590. Match holder/ashtray, 3" tall, 5½" wide, green mark #47, $275.00 – 350.00.

Jugs, Steins & Mugs

Plate 3591. Whiskey jug, 7½" tall, green mark #47, $800.00 – 900.00.

Plate 3592. Wine jug, 8" tall, green mark #47, $900.00 – 1,000.00.

Plate 3593. Whiskey jug, 5¾" tall, green mark #47, $750.00 – 850.00.

Plate 3594. Stein, 7" tall, green mark #47, $900.00 – 1,000.00.

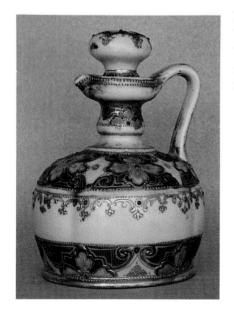

Plate 3595. Whiskey jug, 7¼" tall, blue mark #52, $750.00 – 850.00.

Plate 3596. Mug, 5½" tall, blue mark #47, $300.00 – 400.00.

Plate 3597. Stein, 7¼" tall, green mark #47, $600.00 – 700.00.

Plate 3598. Stein, 7¼" tall, green mark #47, $600.00 – 700.00.

Plate 3599. Stein, 7" tall, green mark #47, $600.00 – 700.00.

Plate 3600. Beverage set, pitcher is 10" tall, blue mark #52, $900.00 – 1,100.00.

Plate 3601. Tankard, 14" tall, unmarked, $750.00 – 900.00.

Plate 3602. Tankard, 17" tall, blue mark #52, $900.00 – 1,100.00.

Plate 3603. Tankard (soft paste style), 12½" tall, mark #91, $300.00 – 400.00. Tankard (soft paste style), 12¼" tall, mark #91, $300.00 – 400.00.

Plate 3604a. Close–up of artist's signature on Plate 3604.

Plate 3605. Mug, 4¾" tall, green mark #47, $300.00 – 400.00.

Plate 3604. Tankard, 12½" tall, gold mark #88, $850.00 – 950.00.

Plate 3606. Mug, 4¾" tall, green mark #47, $250.00 – 300.00.

Plate 3607. Shaving mug, 3¾" tall, green mark #47, $250.00 – 300.00.

Plate 3608. Mug, 5½" tall, green mark #47, $375.00 – 475.00.

Plate 3609. Shaving mug, 3¾" tall, green mark #47, $225.00 – 275.00.

Plate 3610. Tankard, 10½" tall, green mark #47, $700.00 – 800.00.

DRESSER SETS

Plate 3611. Dresser set, mark #229, $275.00 – 350.00.

Plate 3612. Trinket boxes and tray, tray is 4¾" long, box on left is 1¼" tall, box on right 1¾" tall, green mark #47, $60.00 – 80.00.

Plate 3613. Covered box, 7" wide, $175.00 – 225.00.

Plate 3614. Cologne bottle, 4" tall, green mark #47, $150.00 – 200.00.

Plate 3615. Cologne bottle, 4¼" tall, green mark #47, $135.00 – 165.00.

Plate 3616. Cologne bottle, 5" tall, mark #47, $160.00 – 210.00.

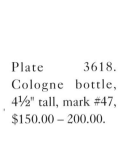

Plate 3617. Cologne bottle, 4½" tall, mark #47, $150.00 – 200.00.

Plate 3618. Cologne bottle, 4½" tall, mark #47, $150.00 – 200.00.

Plate 3619. Trinket box, 5" long, blue mark #52, $100.00 – 140.00.

Plate 3620. Trinket box, 2" long, mark #47, $85.00 – 135.00.

Plate 3621. Two piece hairpin holder, 3¼" tall, blue mark #52, $125.00 – 160.00.

Plate 3622. Talcum powder flask, artist signed, 4¾" tall, blue mark #67, $160.00 – 220.00.

293

Plate 3623. Powder box, 4½" wide, green mark #47, $85.00 – 125.00.

Plate 3624. Stickpin holder, 1½" tall, green mark #52, $150.00 – 200.00.

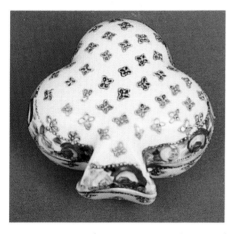

Plate 3625. Trinket box, 3" wide, green mark #52, $85.00 – 135.00.

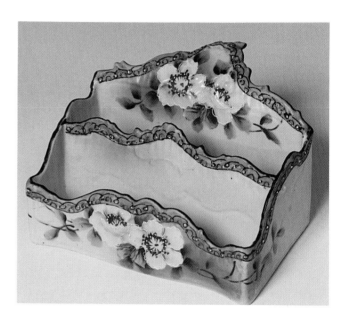

Plate 3626. Letter holder, 7¼" long, mark #4, $275.00 – 325.00.

FERNERS

Plate 3627. Ferner, 7" wide, blue mark #52, $275.00 – 325.00.

Plate 3628. Ferner, 6" wide, blue mark #38, $235.00 – 300.00.

Plate 3629. Ferner, 8" diameter, mark #47, $450.00 – 550.00.

Plate 3630. Pen tray, 8¾" long, green mark #47, $100.00 – 150.00.

Plate 3631. Ferner, 4¾" tall, green mark #47, $200.00 – 250.00.

Plate 3632. Hanging ferner, 5½" wide, green mark #47, $400.00 – 475.00.

Plate 3633. Ferner, 4½" tall, green mark #47, $250.00 – 300.00.

Plate 3634. Hanging ferner, 5½" wide, unmarked, $325.00 – 400.00.

Plate 3635. Ferner, 9½" across handles, green mark #47, $425.00 – 500.00.

Plate 3637. Cracker jar, 8½" tall, blue mark #52, $325.00 – 400.00.

Plate 3636. Cracker jar, 7½" tall, green mark #47, $400.00 – 500.00.

Plate 3638. Cracker jar, 7½" tall, blue mark #52, $325.00 – 400.00.

Plate 3639. Cracker jar, 5" tall, green mark #47, $225.00 – 275.00.

Plate 3640. Cracker jar, 7¾" tall, mark #89, $325.00 – 400.00.

Plate 3641. Cracker jar, 5½" tall, blue mark #52, $275.00 – 450.00.

Plate 3642. Cracker jar, 5" tall, green mark #52, $300.00 – 375.00.

Plate 3643. Cracker jar, 8½" tall, blue mark #47, $250.00 – 300.00.

BOWLS

Plate 3644. Bowl, 6½" wide, green mark #47, $175.00 – 225.00.

Plate 3645. Bowl, 10" wide, green mark #47, $225.00 – 275.00.

Plate 3646. Bowl, 8½" wide, blue mark #52, $250.00 –300.00.

Plate 3647. Bowl, 10¾" wide, blue mark #52, $175.00 – 225.00.

Plate 3648. Bowl, 8½" long, green mark #47, $135.00 – 180.00.

Plate 3649. Bowl, 6¾" wide, green mark #47, $150.00 – 200.00.

Plate 3650. Bowl, 11" diameter, green mark #47, $225.00 – 275.00.

Plate 3651. Bowl, 11" diameter, green mark #47, $225.00 – 275.00.

Plate 3652. Bowl, 7¼" long, green mark #47, $135.00 – 180.00.

Plate 3653. Bowl, 10½" wide, blue mark #25, $235.00 – 300.00.

Plate 3654. Bowl, 8½" wide, mark #47, $150.00 – 200.00.

Plate 3655. Bowl, 8" wide, mark #47, $100.00 – 140.00.

Plate 3656. Bowl, 11" diameter, blue mark #52, $250.00 – 300.00.

Plate 3657. Bowl, 7" wide, green mark #47, $110.00 – 135.00. Bowl, 8" wide, green mark #47, $135.00 – 165.00.

Plate 3658. Bowl, 7" wide, green mark #47, $110.00 – 135.00.

Plate 3659. Bowl, 8" wide, green mark #47, $135.00 – 165.00. Bowl, 8" wide, green mark #47, $135.00 – 165.00.

MISCELLANEOUS
KITCHEN

Plate 3661. Berry bowl set, master bowl is 9¾" wide, mark #6, $250.00 – 300.00.

Plate 3660. Candlestick, 8¼" tall, blue mark #52, $175.00 – 225.00.

Plate 3662. Bowl, 7½" long, blue mark #52, $150.00 – 200.00.

Plate 3663. Covered jar, 5½" tall, green mark #47, $160.00 – 225.00.

Plate 3664. Bowl, 10" diameter, green mark #52, $250.00 – 300.00.

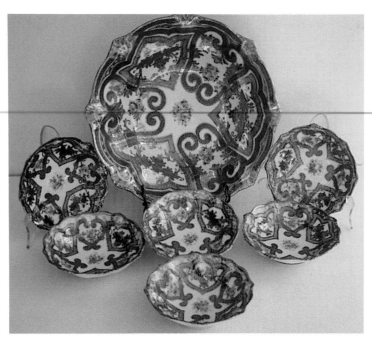

Plate 3665. Berry bowl set, master bowl is 10" in diameter, green mark #52, $300.00 – 400.00.

Plate 3666. Bowl, 10¾" wide, blue mark #52, $400.00 – 500.00.

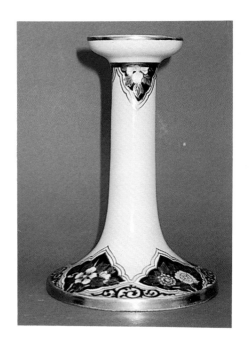

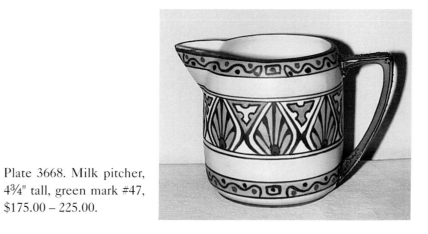

Plate 3668. Milk pitcher, 4¾" tall, green mark #47, $175.00 – 225.00.

Plate 3667. Candlestick, 6¼" tall, green mark #47, $110.00 – 150.00.

Plate 3669. Milk pitcher, 7" tall, mark #80, $175.00 – 225.00.

Plate 3670. Trivet, 6½" wide, green mark #47, $135.00 – 165.00.

Plate 3671. Bowl, 9¾" diameter, mark #81, $165.00 – 225.00.

Plate 3672. Butter dish with underplate, 6½" wide, green mark #47, $150.00 – 200.00.

Plate 3673. Toothpick holder, 2½" tall, mark #80, $60.00 – 85.00.

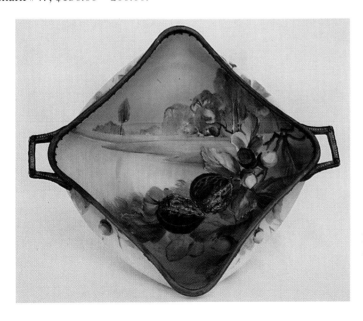

Plate 3674. Bowl, 9¾" long, green mark #47, $125.00 – 160.00.

Plate 3675. Reamer, 4½" across, green mark #47, $175.00 – 225.00. Tea strainer, 6¼" long, blue mark #47, $160.00 – 210.00. Tea strainer, 6" long, green mark #47, $110.00 – 150.00.

Plate 3676. Invalid feeder, 7" long, incised mark #55, $135.00 – 175.00.

Plate 3677. Toothpick holder, 3" tall, green mark #47, $85.00 – 125.00.

Plate 3678. Bowl, 10¼" wide, blue mark #52, $110.00 – 150.00.

Plate 3679. Trivet, 6" wide, red mark #47, $100.00 – 150.00. Trivet, 6" wide, mark #84, $100.00 – 150.00.

Plate 3680. Individual salt and pepper in one unit, mark #47, $200.00 – 250.00. Individual salt and pepper in one unit, mark #54, $200.00 – 250.00.

Plate 3681. Bouillon cup/saucer (saucer is 6" wide), green mark #52, $175.00 – 225.00.

Plate 3682. Loving cup, 6" tall, green mark #47, $200.00 – 250.00.

Plate 3683. Toothpick holder, 3" tall, green mark #47, $70.00 – 90.00.

Plate 3684. Nut set, master bowl is 6¼" wide, green mark #47, $200.00 – 275.00.

Plate 3685. Cake set, master cake plate is 11¼" wide, blue mark #38, $275.00 – 350.00.

Plate 3686. Cake plate, 10¼" wide, green mark #52, $325.00 – 400.00.

Plate 3687. Cake plate, 11½" wide, blue mark #52, $275.00 – 325.00.

Plate 3688. Condiment set, green mark #47, $200.00 – 250.00.

Plate 3689. Milk pitcher, 8¼" tall, green mark #47, $250.00 – 300.00.

Plate 3690. Mustard jar, 4½" tall, blue mark #52, $125.00 – 160.00.

307

Plate 3691. Nut set, master bowl is 6½" wide, green mark #47, $200.00 – 275.00.

Plate 3692. Trivet, 6" wide, green mark #47, $135.00 – 165.00.

Plate 3693. Gravy/sauce dish, 6¼" long, blue mark #52, $150.00 – 200.00.

Plate 3694. Basket dish, 5" long, blue mark #52, $125.00 – 160.00.

Plate 3695. Egg server, 6½" wide, mark #84, $135.00 – 175.00.

Plate 3696. Cake plate, 10¾" wide, unmarked, $225.00 – 300.00.

Plate 3697. Cake plate, 11½" wide, blue
mark #52, $275.00 – 350.00.

Plate 3698. Pair of napkin holders, unmarked, $140.00 – 200.00 pair.

Plate 3699. Plate, 9" wide, mark removed,
$80.00 – 110.00.

Plate 3700. Gravy/sauce dish with ladle, 7" long, green mark
#47, $200.00 – 275.00.

Plate 3701. Candlestick lamp, 12" tall, green mark #47, $1,600.00 – 1,900.00.

Plate 3702. Lamp, base is 10½" tall, blue mark #52, $350.00 – 450.00.

Plate 3703. Lamp, 9½" tall, mark u n k n o w n , $125.00 – 160.00.

Plate 3704. Pair of lamps, mark unknown, $600.00 – 700.00 pair.

Plate 3705. Toothpick holders with attached tray, top row: 5" long, blue mark #40; 5" long, green mark #10; middle row: 5" long, blue mark #67; 5" long, blue mark #52; 5" long, blue mark #92; bottom row: 5" long, green mark #47, 5" long, green mark #47, and 5" long, blue mark #92, $65.00 – 110.00 each.

Plate 3706. Pair of covered jars, 7¾" tall, green mark #47, $165.00 – 225.00

Plate 3707. Wall pocket, 9" long, green mark #47, $235.00 – 300.00.

Plate 3708. Punchbowl set, two piece bowl, 16" wide, ten individual pedestalled cups, green mark #47, $2,200.00 – 2,600.00.

Plate 3709. Game plates, 7¾" wide, mark #103, $150.00 – 200.00 each.

Plate 3710. Game set, green mark #47, $2,200.00 – 2,600.00.

CONDENSED MILK CONTAINERS

Plate 3712. Condensed milk container, 6" tall, blue mark #52, $225.00 – 275.00.

Plate 3711. Condensed milk container, (note: this is the genuine pattern that the new fake items have copied), mark #81, $225.00 – $275.00.

Plate 3714. Condensed milk container, blue mark #84, $175.00 – 225.00.

Plate 3713. Jam jar, 5½" tall, unmarked, $125.00 – 160.00.

Plate 3715. Condensed milk container, green mark #47, $175.00 – 225.00.

Plate 3716. Condensed milk container, blue mark #103, $175.00 – 225.00.

Plate 3717. Condensed milk container, (white and gold pattern), blue mark #103, $175.00 – 225.00.

Plate 3718. Condensed milk container, blue mark #103, $175.00 – 225.00.

Plate 3719. Condensed milk container, red mark #47, $175.00 – 225.00.

Plate 3720. Condensed milk container, blue mark #103, $175.00 – 225.00.

Plate 3721. Condensed milk container, blue mark #103, $175.00 – 225.00.

Plate 3722. Condensed milk container, mark #80, $175.00 – 225.00.

Plate 3723. Condensed milk container, blue mark #52, $200.00 – 250.00.

Plate 3724. Condensed milk container, red mark #47, $175.00 – 225.00.

Plate 3725. Condensed milk container, red mark #47, $175.00 – 225.00.

Plate 3726. Condensed milk container, green mark #47, $175.00 – 225.00.

Plate 3727. Condensed milk container, green mark #47, $175.00 – 225.00.

Plate 3728. Condensed milk container, green mark #47, $175.00 – 225.00.

Plate 3729. Condensed milk container, green mark #47, $175.00 – 225.00.

Plate 3730. Condensed milk container, green mark #47, $175.00 – 225.00.

Plate 3731. Condensed milk container, green mark #47, $175.00 – 225.00.

Plate 3732. Condensed milk container, mark #80, $175.00 – 225.00.

Plate 3733. Condensed milk container, green mark #47, $175.00 – 225.00.

Plate 3734. Condensed milk container, red mark #47, $175.00 – 225.00.

Plate 3735. Condensed milk container, green mark #47, $175.00 – 225.00.

Plate 3736. Condensed milk container, green mark #47, $175.00 – 225.00.

Plate 3737. Condensed milk container, green mark #47, $175.00 – 225.00.

Plate 3738. Condensed milk container, red mark #47, $175.00 – 225.00.

TEA SETS

Plate 3739. Tea set, teapot, green mark #47; creamer and sugar bowl, mark #27, $375.00 – 475.00.

Plate 3740. Tea set, teapot, creamer, sugar bowl, eight cups and saucers, unmarked, $850.00 – 1,000.00.

Plate 3741. Tea set, four cups and saucers, pot is 5½" tall, green mark #47, $475.00 – 550.00.

Plate 3742. Tea set, four cups and saucers, blue mark #47, $650.00 – 750.00.

Plate 3743. Tea set, six cups and saucers, blue mark #52, $1,000.00 – 1,200.00.

Plate 3744. Tea set, four cups and saucers, blue mark #47, $475.00 – 550.00.

Plate 3745. Tea set, six cups and saucers, blue mark #7, $425.00 – 500.00.

Plate 3746. Set of four cups and saucers, unmarked, $200.00 – 275.00 set.

Plate 3747. Tea set, five cups and saucers, mark #80, $475.00 – 550.00.

Chocolate Sets

Plate 3748. Chocolate set, five cups and saucers, blue mark #4, $500.00 – 600.00.

Plate 3749. Chocolate set, six cups and saucers, condensed milk container, blue mark #52, $725.00 – 800.00.

Plate 3750. Chocolate set, four cups and saucers, blue mark #52, $1,000.00 – 1,200.00.

Plate 3751. Chocolate set, six cups and saucers, blue mark #47, $1,200.00 – 1,400.00.

Plate 3752. Chocolate set, four cups and saucers, green mark #47, $1,100.00 – 1,300.00.

Plate 3753. Chocolate set, six cups and saucers, mark removed, $900.00 – 1,100.00.

Plate 3754. Chocolate set, six cups and saucers, green mark #47, $650.00 – 750.00.

Plate 3755. Chocolate set, four cups and saucers, green mark #47, $700.00 – 825.00.

Plate 3756. Chocolate set, six cups and saucers, blue mark #4, $500.00 – 600.00.

Plate 3757. Chocolate set, four cups and saucers, blue mark #70, $750.00 – 900.00.

Plate 3759. Chocolate set, six cups and saucers, green mark #47, $850.00 – 950.00.

Plate 3758. Chocolate set, six cups and saucers, green mark #47, $500.00 – 600.00.

Plate 3760. Chocolate set, four cups and saucers, green mark #47, $400.00 – 500.00.

Plate 3761. Chocolate set, six cups and saucers, green mark #47, $400.00 – 500.00.

Plate 3762. Chocolate set, six cups and saucers, green mark #47, $500.00 – 600.00.

Plate 3763. Chocolate set, four cups and saucers, green mark #81, $650.00 – 750.00.

Plate 3764. Chocolate set, six cups and saucers, blue mark #52, $650.00 – 750.00.

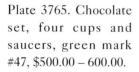

Plate 3765. Chocolate set, four cups and saucers, green mark #47, $500.00 – 600.00.

Plate 3766. Chocolate set, four cups and saucers, blue mark #71, $450.00 – 550.00.

Plate 3767. Chocolate set, four cups and saucers, green mark #47, $650.00 – 750.00.

Plate 3768. Creamer and sugar bowl, mark #52, $135.00 – 175.00.

Plate 3769. Chocolate set, comes with six cups and saucers, blue mark #52, $750.00 – 850.00.

Plate 3770. Chocolate pot, 10" tall, green mark #7, $125.00 – 160.00.

Plate 3771. Demitasse set, pot is 6" tall, green mark #47, $300.00 – 375.00.

Plate 3772. Tea set, pot is 7" tall, mark #25, $500.00 – 600.00.

Plate 3773. Demitasse set, four cups and saucers, pot is 6¼" tall, green mark #47, $350.00 – 450.00.

Plate 3775. Demitasse set, six cups and saucers, pot is 7" tall, serving tray and creamer and sugar bowl, green mark #47, $875.00 – 1,000.00.

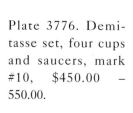

Plate 3774. Demitasse set with matching tray, green mark #47, $350.00 – 425.00.

Plate 3776. Demitasse set, four cups and saucers, mark #10, $450.00 – 550.00.

Plate 3778. Demitasse set, four cups and saucers, blue mark #52, $675.00 – 800.00.

Plate 3777. Demitasse set, six cups and saucers, blue mark #47, $400.00 – 500.00.

DOLLS

Plate 3779. Child's feeding dish, molded in relief, mark #84, $160.00 – 225.00.

Plate 3780. Doll, 25" tall, mark #236, $425.00 – 500.00.

Plate 3781. Doll, 4" tall, mark #55, $135.00 – 175.00.

Plate 3782. Doll, 21" tall, mark #128, $350.00 – 425.00.

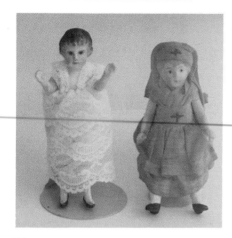

Plate 3783. Doll, 6" tall, mark #55, $140.00 – 185.00. Doll, 5¾" tall, original WWI Red Cross uniform, mark #55, $180.00 – 225.00.

Plate 3784. Doll, 4½" tall, mark #55, $150.00 – 190.00.

Plate 3785. Doll, 4" tall, mark #55, $160.00 – 200.00.

Plate 3786. Doll, 5" tall, mark #55, $150.00 – 190.00.

Plate 3788. Doll, 14" tall, mark #260, $300.00 – 375.00.

Plate 3787. Doll, 17" tall, mark #259, $325.00 – 400.00.

Plate 3789. Doll, 15" tall, mark # 1 7 3 , $300.00 – 375.00.

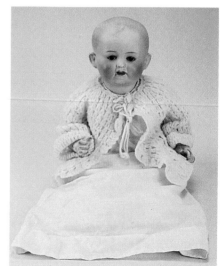

Plate 3790. Doll, 16" tall, mark #131, $300.00 – 375.00.

Glossary

American Indian design – a popular collectible in Nippon porcelain; these designs include the Indian in a canoe, Indian warrior, Indian hunting wild game, and the Indian maiden.

Apricot (ume) – in Japan, stands for strength and nobility, is also a symbol of good luck.

Art Deco – a style of decoration which hit its peak in Europe and America around 1925 although items were manufactured with this decor as early as 1910. The style was modernistic; geometric patterns were popular. Motifs used were shapes such as circles, rectangles, cylinders, and cones.

Art Nouveau – the name is derived from the French words, meaning "new art." During the period of 1885 – 1925, artists tended to use bolder colors, and realism was rejected. Free–flowing designs were used, breaking away from the imitations of the past.

Artist signed – items signed by the artist, most appear to be of English extraction, probably painted during the heyday of hand painting chinaware at the turn of the century.

Azalea pattern – pattern found on Nippon items, pink azaleas with green to gray leaves and gold rims. Nippon-marked pieces match the Noritake-marked Azalea pattern items. The Azalea pattern was originally offered by the Larkin Co. to its customers as premiums.

Backstamp – mark found on Nippon porcelain items identifying the manufacturer, exporter or importer, and country of origin.

Bamboo tree – in Japan, symbolic of strength, faithfulness, and honesty, also a good luck symbol. The bamboo resists the storm but it yields to it and rises again.

Beading – generally a series of clay dots applied on Nippon porcelain, very often enameled over in gold. Later Nippon pieces merely had dots of enameling.

Biscuit – clay which has been fired but not glazed.

Bisque – same as biscuit, term also used by collectors to describe a matte finish on an item.

Blank – greenware or bisque items devoid of decoration.

Blown–out items – this term is used by collectors and dealers for items that have a molded relief pattern embossed on by the mold in which the article was shaped. It is not actually "blown–out" as the glass items are, but the pattern is raised from the item. (See molded relief items.)

Bottger, Johann F. – a young German alchemist who supposedly discovered the value of kaolin in making porcelain. This discovery helped to revolutionize the china making industry in Europe beginning in the early 1700s.

Carp – fish that symbolizes strength and perseverance.

Casting – the process of making reproductions by pouring slip into molds.

Cha no yu – Japanese tea ceremony.

Chargers – archaic term for large platters or plates.

Cheese hard clay – same as leather hard clay.

Cherry blossoms – national flower of Japan and emblem of the faithful warrior.

Ching–te–Chen – ancient city in China where nearly a million people lived and worked with almost all devoted to the making of porcelain.

Chrysanthemum – depicts health and longevity, the crest of the emperor of Japan. The chrysanthemum blooms late in the year and lives longer than other flowers.

Citron – stands for wealth.

Cloisonné on Porcelain – on Nippon porcelain wares it resembles the other cloisonné pieces except that it was produced on a porcelain body instead of metal. The decoration is divided into cells called cloisons. These cloisons were divided by strips of metal wire which kept the colors separated during the firing.

Cobalt oxide – blue oxide imported to Japan after 1868 for decoration of wares. Gosu, a pebble found in Oriental riverbeds, had previously been used but was scarce and more expensive than the imported oxide. Cobalt oxide is the most powerful of all the coloring oxides for tinting.

Coralene items – were made by firing small colorless beads on the wares. Many are signed Kinran, US Patent, NBR 912171, February 9, 1909, Japan. Tiny glass beads had previously been applied to glass items in the shapes of birds, flowers, leaves, etc. and no doubt this was an attempt to copy it. Japanese coralene was patented by Alban L. Rock, an American living in Yokohama, Japan. The vitreous coating of beads gave the item a plush velvety look. The beads were permanently fired on and gave a luminescence to the design. The most popular design had been one of seaweed and coral, hence the name coralene was given to this type of design.

Crane – a symbol of good luck in Japan, also stands for marital fidelity and is an emblem of longevity.

Daffodil – a sign of spring to the Japanese.

Decalcomania – a process of transferring a wet paper print onto the surface of an item. It was made to resemble hand-painted work.

Deer – stands for divine messenger.

Diaper pattern – repetitive pattern of small design used on Nippon porcelain, often geometric or floral.

Dragons (ryu) – a symbol of strength, goodness, and good fortune. The Japanese dragon has three claws and was thought to reside in the sky. Clouds, water, and lightning often accompany the dragon. The dragon is often portrayed in high relief using the slip trailing method of decor.

Drain mold – a mold used in making hollow ware. Liquid slip is poured into the mold until the desired thickness of the walls is achieved. The excess clay is poured out. When the item starts to shrink away from the mold, it is removed.

Drape mold – or flopover mold, used to make flat bottomed items. Moist clay is rolled out and draped over the mold. It is then pressed firmly into shape.

Dutch scenes – popular on Nippon items, include those of windmills, and men and women dressed in Dutch costumes.

Edo – or Yedo, the largest city in Japan, later renamed Tokyo, meaning eastern capital.

Embossed design – see molded relief.

Enamel beading – dots of enameling painted by the artist in gold or other colors and often made to resemble jewels, such as emeralds and rubies. Many times this raised beading will be found in brown or black colors.

Fairings – items won or bought at fairs as souvenirs.

Feldspar – most common rock found on earth.

Fern leaves – symbolic of ample good fortune.

Fettles or Mold Marks – ridges formed where sections of molds are joined at the seam. These fettles have to be removed before the item is decorated.

Finial – the top knob on a cover of an item, used to lift off the cover.

Firing – the cooking or baking of clay ware.

Flopover mold – same as drape mold.

Flux – an ingredient added to glaze to assist in making the item fire properly. It causes the glaze to melt at a specified temperature.

Glaze – composed of silica, alumina, and flux, and is applied to porcelain pieces. During the firing process, the glaze joins with the clay item to form a glasslike surface. It seals the pores and makes the item impervious to liquids.

Gold trim – has to be fired at lower temperatures or the gold would sink into the enameled decoration. If overfired, the gold becomes discolored.

Gouda ceramics – originally made in Gouda, a province of south Holland. These items were copied on the Nippon wares and were patterned after the Art Nouveau style.

Gosu – pebble found in Oriental riverbeds, a natural cobalt. It was used to color items until 1868 when oxidized cobalt was introduced into Japan.

Greenware – clay which has been molded but not fired.

Hard paste porcelain – paste meaning the body of substance, porcelain being made from clay using kaolin. This produces a hard translucent body when fired.

Ho–o bird – sort of a bird of paradise who resides on earth and is associated with the empress of Japan. Also see phoenix bird.

Incised backstamp – the backstamp marking is scratched into the surface of a clay item.

Incised decoration – a sharp tool or stick was used to produce the design right onto the body of the article while it was still in a state of soft clay.

Iris – the Japanese believe this flower wards off evil; associated with warriors because of its sword–like leaves.

Jasper Ware – see Wedgwood.

Jigger – a machine resembling a potter's wheel. Soft pliable clay is placed onto a convex revolving mold. As the wheel turns, a template is held against it, trimming off the excess clay on the outside. The revolving mold shapes the inside of the item and the template cuts the outside.

Jolley – a machine like a jigger only in reverse. The revolving mold is concave and the template forms the inside of the item. The template is lowered inside the revolving mold. The mold forms the outside surface while the template cuts the inside.

Jomon – neolithic hunters and fishermen in Japan dating back to approximately 2500 B.C. Their pottery was hand formed and marked with an overall rope or cord pattern. It was made of unwashed clay, unglazed, and was baked in open fires.

Kaga – province in Japan.

Kaolin – highly refractory clay and one of the principal ingredients used in making porcelain. It is a pure white residual clay, a decomposition of granite.

Kao–ling – Chinese word meaning "the high hills," the word kaolin is derived from it.

Kiln – oven in which pottery is fired.

Leather hard clay – clay which is dry enough to hold its shape but still damp and moist, no longer in a plastic state, also called cheese hard.

Liquid slip – clay in a liquid state.

Lobster – symbol of long life.

Luster decoration – a metallic type of coloring decoration, gives an iridescent effect.

Matte finish – also "mat" and "matt." A dull glaze having a low reflectance when fired.

McKinley Tariff Act of 1890 – Chapter 1244, Section 6 states "That on and after the first day of March, eighteen hundred and ninety–one, all articles of foreign manufacture, such as are usually or ordinarily marked, stamped, branded, or labeled, and all packages containing such or other imported articles, shall, respectively, be plainly marked, stamped, branded, or labeled in legible English words, so as to indicate the country of their origin; and unless so marked, stamped, branded, or labeled, they shall not be admitted to entry."

Meiji period – period of 1868 – 1912 in Japan when Emperor Mutsuhito reigned. It means "enlightened rule."

Middle East scenes – designs used on Nippon pieces, featuring pyramids, deserts, palm trees, and riders on camels.

Model – the shape from which the mold is made.

Molded relief items – the pattern is embossed on the item by the mold in which the article is shaped. These items give the appearance that the pattern is caused by some type of upward pressure from the underside. Collectors often refer to these items as "blown–out."

Molds – contain a cavity in which castings are made. They are generally made from plaster of Paris and are used for shaping clay objects. Both liquid and plastic clay may be used. The mold can also be made of clay or rubber, however, plaster was generally used as it absorbed moisture immediately from the clay. Raised ornamentation may also be formed directly in the mold.

Moriage – refers to liquid clay (slip) relief decoration. On Nippon items this was usually done by "slip trailing" or hand rolling and shaping the clay on an item.

Morimura Bros. – importers of Japanese wares in the United States and the sole importers of Noritake wares. It was opened in New York City in 1876 and closed in 1941.

Mutsuhito – Emperor of Japan from 1868 – 1912. His reign was called the Meiji period which meant enlightened rule.

Nagoya – a large city in Japan, location of Noritake Co.

Narcissus – stands for good fortune.

Ningyo – Japanese name for doll, meaning human being and image.

Nippon – the name the Japanese people called their country. It comes from a Chinese phrase meaning "the source of the sun" and sounds like Neehon in Japanese.

Noritake Co. – This company produced more than 90 percent of the Nippon era wares that now exist. Their main office is located in Nagoya, Japan.

Orchid – means hidden beauty and modesty to the Japanese.

Overglaze decoration – a design is either painted or a decal applied to an item which already has a fired glazed surface. The article is then refired to make the decoration permanent.

Pattern stamping – the design was achieved by using a special stamp or a plaster roll having the design cut into it. The design was pressed into the soft clay body of an item.

Paulownia flower – crest of the empress of Japan.

Peach – stands for marriage.

Peacock – stands for elegance and beauty.

Peony – considered the king of flowers in Japan.

Perry, Matthew, Comm., USN – helped to fashion the Kanagawa treaty in 1854 between the United States and Japan. This treaty opened the small ports of Shimoda and Hakodate to trade. Shipwrecked sailors were also to receive good treatment and an American consul was permitted to reside at Shimoda.

Petuntse – clay found in felspathic rocks such as granite. Its addition to porcelain made the item more durable. Petuntse is also called china stone.

Phoenix bird – sort of bird of paradise which resides on earth and is associated with the empress of Japan. This bird appears to be a cross between a peacock, a pheasant, and a gamecock. There appear to be many designs for this bird as each artist had his own conception of how it should look. It is also a symbol to the Japanese of all that is beautiful.

Pickard Co. – a china decorating studio originally located in Chicago. This firm decorated blank wares imported from a number of countries including Nippon.

Pine tree – to the Japanese this tree is symbolic of friendship and prosperity and depicts the winter season. It is also a sign of good luck and a sign of strength.

Plastic clay – clay in a malleable state, able to be shaped and formed without collapsing.

Plum – stands for womanhood. Plum blossoms reflect bravery.

Porcelain – a mixture composed mainly of kaolin and petuntse which is fired at a high temperature and vitrified.

Porcelain slip – porcelain clay in a liquid form.

Porcellaine – French adaptation of the word "porcelain."

Porcellana – Italian word meaning cowry shell. The Chinese ware which was brought back to Venice in the fifteenth century was thought to resemble the cowry shell and was called porcellana.

Portrait items – items decorated with portraits, many of European beauties. Some appear to be hand painted, most are decal work.

Potter's wheel – rotating device onto which a ball of plastic clay is placed. The wheel is turned and the potter molds the clay with his hands and is capable of producing cylindrical objects.

Pottery – in its broadest sense, includes all forms of wares made from clay.

Press mold – used to make handles, finials, figurines, etc. A two–piece mold into which soft clay is placed. The two pieces are pressed together to form items.

Relief – molded (See molded relief items).

Royal Crockery – name of Nippon pieces marked with RC on backstamp.

Satsuma – a sea-going principality in Japan, an area where many of the old famous kilns are found, and also a type of Japanese ware. Satsuma is a cream-colored glazed pottery which is finely crackled.

Slip – liquid clay.

Slip trailing – a process where liquid clay was applied to porcelain via tubing or a cone-shaped device made of paper with a metal tip. A form of painting but with clay instead of paint. The slip is often applied quite heavily and gives a thick, raised appearance.

Slurry – thick slip.

Solid casting mold – used for shallow type items such as bowls and plates. In this type of mold, the thickness of the walls is determined by the mold and every piece is formed identically. The mold shapes both the inside and the outside of the piece and the thickness of the walls can be controlled. Solid casting can be done with either liquid or plastic clay.

Sometsuke style decoration – items decorated with an underglaze of blue and white colors.

Sprigging – the application of small molded relief decoration to the surface of porcelain by use of liquid clay as in Jasper Ware.

Sprig mold – a one–piece mold used in making ornaments. Clay is fitted or poured into a mold which is incised with a design. Only one side is molded and the exposed side becomes the back of the finished item.

Taisho – name of the period reigned over by Emperor Yoshihito in Japan from 1912 – 1926. It means "great peace."

Tapestry – a type of decor used on Nippon porcelain. A cloth was dipped into liquid slip and then stretched onto the porcelain item. During the bisque firing, the material burned off and left a textured look on the porcelain piece, resembling needlepoint in many cases. The item was then painted and fired again in the usual manner.

Template – profile of the pattern being cut.

Throwing – the art of forming a clay object on a potter's wheel.

Tiger (tora) – a symbol of longevity.

Transfer print – see Decalcomania.

Translucent – not transparent but clear enough to allow rays of light to pass through.

Ultraviolet lamp – lamp used to detect cracks and hidden repairs in items.

Underglaze decoration – this type of decoration is applied on bisque china (fired once), then the item is glazed and fired again.

Victorian Age design – decor used on some Nippon pieces, gaudy and extremely bold colors used.

Vitreous – glass–like.

Vitrify – to change into a glasslike substance due to the application of heat.

Wasters – name given to pieces ruined or marred in the kiln.

Water lilies – represent autumn in Japan.

Wedgwood – term used to refer to Nippon pieces which attempt to imitate Josiah Wedgwood's Jasper Ware. The items usually have a light blue background. The Nippon pieces were generally produced with a slip trailing decor however, rather than the sprigging ornamentation made popular by Wedgwood. White clay slip was trailed onto the background color of the item by use of tubing or a cone-shaped device to form the pattern.

Yamato – district in central Japan.

Yayoi – people of the bronze and iron culture in Japan dating back to 300 – 100 B.C. They were basically an agricultural people. They made pottery using the potter's wheel.

Yedo – or Edo, the largest city in Japan, renamed Tokyo, meaning eastern capital.

Yoshihito – Emperor of Japan from 1912 – 1926. He took the name of Taisho which meant "great peace."

Alden, Aimee Neff. *Collector's Encyclopedia of Early Noritake*. Collector Books, Paducah, Ky., 1995.

Bowman, Leslie Greene. *American Arts And Crafts, Virtue In Design*. Bulfinch/Little, Brown & Co., Boston, Toronto, London, 1990.

Butler Brothers catalogs, 1907, 1908, 1909, 1911, 1912, 1917, 1918, 1919, 1920.

Ceramic Art catalog, circa 1904.

Coleman, Dorothy, S. Elizabeth, A. and Evelyn, J. *The Collector's Encyclopedia of Dolls*. Crown Publishers, Inc., New York, N.Y., 1968.

Duncan, Alastair and deBarthe, Georges. *Glass by Gallé*. Harry N. Abrams, Inc. Publishers, New York, N.Y., 1984.

Garner, Philippe. *Emile Gallé*. St. Martin's Press, New York, N.Y., 1976.

Jewel Ways, 1916 – 1919.

Larkin catalog, 1916.

Masias, Marie-Therese and Pinkas-Massin, Agnes. *Painting on China*. Arco Publishing Inc., New York, N.Y., 1984.

Sensior, Albert. *Jean-Francois Millet*. James R. Osgood and Co., New York, N.Y., 1881.

Southwell, Sheila. *China Painting Projects Around The World*. Sterling Publication Co., Inc., New York, N.Y., 1991.

——————— *Painting China and Porcelain*. Blandford Press Ltd., Poole, Dorset, U.K., 1980.

Van Patten, Joan, F. *Collector's Encyclopedia of Nippon Porcelain*. Collector Books, Paducah, KY., 1979.

———————*Collector's Encyclopedia of Nippon Porcelain, Second Series*. Collector Books, Paducah, Ky., 1982.

———————*Collector's Encyclopedia of Nippon Porcelain, Third Series*. Collector Books, Paducah, Ky., 1986.

———————*Collector's Encyclopedia of Nippon Porcelain, Fourth Series*. Collector Books, Paducah, Ky., 1997.

———————*Price Guide for Collector's Encyclopedia of Nippon Porcelain*. Collector Books, Paducah, Ky., 1994.

Volpe, Tod, M., Cathers, Beth, Duncan, Alastair. *Treasures of the American Arts and Crafts Movement, 1890 – 1920*. Harry N. Abrams, Inc. Publishers, New York, N.Y., 1988.

Warmus, William. *Emile Gallé, Dreams Into Glass*. The Corning Museum of Glass, Corning, N.Y., 1984.

Index

Items are listed by Plate numbers in this book.

335